Nothing
but
Newborn

A First-month
Primer for Parents

Janet A. Stockheim, MD, MPH, FAAP

ISBN: 1-4196-8729-8
ISBN-13: 9781419687297

Library of Congress Control Number: 2008900228
Visit www.booksurge.com to order additional copies.

ABOUT THE AUTHOR

Janet A. Stockheim, MD, MPH, FAAP, has been caring for newborns and educating new parents for nearly two decades. She earned her medical and public health degrees from New York Medical College and completed a residency in pediatrics at Westchester County Medical Center in Valhalla, New York. She received additional training in pediatric infectious diseases at Children's Memorial Hospital of Northwestern University in Chicago, Illinois. As the Pediatric Infectious Disease Specialist for the School Health Program at the New York City Department of Health, she served as a citywide medical and educational resource for several years. She is currently an assistant professor of pediatrics at New York Medical College and continues to teach medical students, residents, other health professionals, and parents. She also provides general pediatric care to newborns and infants in Westchester County, New York. She is a national medical honor society member, a fellow of the American Academy of Pediatrics, and has received multiple awards and recognition throughout her training and her career for commitment to children and teaching excellence. Her publications include chapters in medical textbooks, original research published in medical journals, and newsletter entries. She lives in Westchester County, New York, with her husband and three children.

To my husband, Kerry, and our newborns-no-longer, Rachel, Jack, and Brendan.

TABLE OF CONTENTS

1
INTRODUCTION

There is nothing in the world quite like a newborn—nothing as amazing as conception, nothing as anticipated and unique as the appearance of two individuals blended together, and nothing as momentous as the day each of us was born. There is also nothing as predictable as a newborn baby's parts, needs and functions, and new parents' questions and anxieties. This book is full of nothing but newborn information, from the time of birth through the first month. Within that time, you may change 180 (or more) diapers and feed and burp your baby 240 (or more) times, and you *will* survive thirty sleepless nights in a row. With that much practice, it is likely that you will develop confidence and expertise in your new role. You will establish daily routines that work for you and your baby, and you will become familiar with your baby's every nuance and feature. In that time, your baby will also begin to develop unique characteristics that reflect his temperament and your parenting. Your newborn will grow up, and you will enjoy *almost* every minute of it.

This book is intended to guide parents through understanding and caring for a typical healthy newborn. Specific questions or concerns about your particular baby should, of course, be directed to your pediatrician or health care provider.

2
STANDARD CARE AFTER DELIVERY

Soon after delivery, a health professional familiar with newborns should examine your baby. In the United States, several procedures are included in the standard care of newborns:

1. Apgar scores in the range of one (worst) to ten (best) will be assigned to your baby at one minute and five minutes after birth. Scores are based on color, heart rate, breathing effort, muscle tone, and reaction to stimulation. Each category earns up to two points. Most babies receive a score of eight or nine; a score of ten is uncommon, as most babies have purple coloring of their hands and feet at birth. A score less than seven may indicate the need for further monitoring and evaluation.

2. Medicated eye drops are placed in your baby's eyes at the time of birth. These drops protect against infections (gonorrhea and chlamydia), which can pass from mother to baby if present at the time of delivery.

3. A vitamin K injection into your baby's thigh protects against a serious bleeding disorder in newborns.

4. State newborn screening programs collect drops of blood taken from your baby's heel to detect certain inherited diseases very early in life. The list of diseases included in the screening program varies by state. You can contact your state's health department for a list of disorders included in its newborn screening program.

5. In the United States, the recommendation is to administer the first dose of **hepatitis B vaccine** to all babies at the time of delivery. It is especially important for your baby to receive this vaccine if the mother is infected with hepatitis B virus. This vaccine requires your consent, and the nursery staff should discuss this with you.

6. Your newborn's **blood type** may be checked at the time of delivery and compared to the mother's blood type. If an infant's blood type differs too much from the mother's, the infant's blood may break down partially. This process may lead to *jaundice* (yellowing of the skin) and/or anemia (a low red blood cell count).

7. Your baby may have a **hearing test** performed during the nursery stay.

8. Your baby will be **weighed and measured** and vital signs (heart rate, breathing rate, temperature and blood pressure) will be monitored.

9. Your baby will be observed throughout the nursery stay for **jaundice**, which is common in healthy newborns. This may include checking blood levels of bilirubin, the substance responsible for the yellow discoloration of the skin.

10. Most hospital nurseries have a security system in place to track each baby's whereabouts and prevent abductions. A small **tracking device** may be attached to your baby's ankle or umbilical clip, which will trigger an alarm if it approaches an exit. These clips should be removed or deactivated before your baby is discharged from the hospital.

11. Other procedures or screening tests may be performed on your baby depending on the policies of the state or facility in which your child is born.

3
NORMAL PARTS AND VARIATIONS

Head

At birth, your baby's head may have a round or elongated shape. Newborn skull bones are moveable and connected to each other by fibrous connections called "sutures." This mobility allows for passage through the narrow birth canal and accommodates future brain growth. These sutures feel like long thin spaces or raised ridges along the edges of the bones. There is a round space, the "soft spot," where several sutures meet at the front of the head called the "fontanel" (see figure). Passage through the birth canal or normal compression in the womb during labor may cause the head to be cone shaped, and hard bumps may be felt if the skull bones overlap at the sutures. Soon after birth, the bones will settle back into a round shape, though the sutures and the fontanel will not close until sometime between six and eighteen months of age. Although the fontanel is normally soft and flat, it may bulge slightly when the baby cries and pulsate with each heartbeat when the baby is at rest.

Occasionally, the trauma of birth also causes bleeding under the skin of the scalp (caput succedaneum) or under the outer membrane of a skull bone (cephalohematoma), which feels like a soft squishy area. It may enlarge over several hours after birth, but should disappear within several weeks.

If the baby's head rests repeatedly in the same position, a flat area may develop on the back or one side of the skull. Resting the baby's head in different positions during sleep, and placing the baby on her tummy as often as possible while awake, will allow the bones of the skull to grow symmetrically.

A baby's head is very large and heavy relative to the rest of the body. Because a baby is born with very weak neck muscles, the head must always be supported.

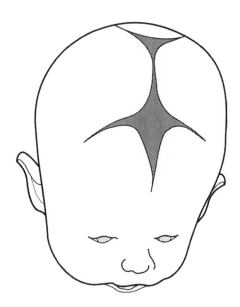

The open bones of the skull meet to form suture lines and an open fontanel or soft spot.

Hair

The amount of hair that covers a baby's head is variable. Some babies are born bald while others have a full head of thick hair. All babies develop with fine, soft hair covering their bodies called "lanugo" hair. This hair is most noticeable in preterm babies and is replaced by short, soft "vellus" hair as babies approach full term.

Eyes

Your baby's eyes should be open at the time of birth, though vision is limited. Newborn eyes can see a distance of approximately twelve inches. The recognizable form of a human face captures their attention, especially during feedings, and objects that are brightly colored or have dark and light contrast are most noticeable to newborn eyes. It is normal for babies to occasionally cross their eyes for the first six months of life.

It is not unusual for babies to have slight differences in the shape or size of their two eyes. Generally, the difference becomes less noticeable as the baby grows over the years. Eyelashes and eyebrows may not be fully noticeable at birth, but should develop over time.

Eye color is not final until the end of the first year of life. Most Caucasian babies begin with blue eyes that may darken over time, whereas babies with darkly pigmented skin often have darkly pigmented eyes from birth.

It is standard practice for newborns to have medicated drops or ointment placed in their eyes at the time of delivery. As a result, your newborn's eyes may appear slightly irritated for one to two days after birth. It is also common for babies to have small areas of bright red bleeding in the whites of their eyes (subconjunctival hemorrhages) along with swelling of the eyelids, which result from the trauma of birth. The hemorrhages generally resolve within several weeks and are of no consequence.

Newborn eyes produce fluid, which lubricates their surface, though they do not produce large tears until several weeks after birth. The lubricating fluid and tears normally drain through small channels (tear ducts) at the inner corners of the eyes leading into the nose. If a channel is blocked, the fluid spills out the front of the eye, causing it to appear watery. This condition (dacryostenosis) is common and generally resolves by the baby's first birthday. The stagnant, overflowing fluid may turn thick if it gathers dust or surface germs, and can be wiped away with a clean, moist cloth. If the eye or the skin around the eye becomes red or swollen, a pediatrician should examine your baby.

Ears

Your baby can hear sounds at birth, and many hospital nurseries now perform hearing tests on newborns to confirm hearing function. Occasionally, residual birth fluid in the ear canals will interfere with the hearing test. If your baby "fails," a repeat test should be scheduled.

Your baby's outer ears are made of cartilage and are very soft and springy. Over several months, the cartilage will harden into a permanent shape. Some babies have a small "pit" in the skin in front of the top of the ear on one or both sides. These "pre-auricular pits" are normal and often seen in other family members.

Piercing newborn ears is not recommended. If you are determined to pierce your baby's ears during infancy, most pediatricians recommend waiting until the baby is immunized against tetanus, a serious infection that enters the body through broken skin. Tetanus vaccines are given to babies at two months, four months, and six months of age. After three doses, a baby is well protected against tetanus.

Nose

Babies are able to smell at birth and can soon recognize their mother's scent and the smell of her milk. A baby also depends on its nose for breathing, and a baby who cannot breathe through the nose will have great difficulty feeding and sleeping. Since babies develop in a liquid environment before birth, it is common practice to suction fluid out of a baby's nose at the time of delivery. You may continue to notice fluid or congestion in your baby's nose for several weeks after birth, especially if your baby tends to spit up milk. Accumulated mucous and residual milk can be loosened with unmedicated normal saline nose drops and removed with a bulb syringe (see "nasal congestion" in the troubleshooting chapter).

If your baby is unable or unwilling to feed easily because of difficulty breathing through the nose, you should consult your pediatrician.

Mouth

Your baby's mouth is used primarily for feeding and sucking. Babies suck while they are developing in utero, and a thumb-sucking baby may actually be born with a "sucking" blister on its upper lip or hand.

Since a newborn's diet is liquid, teeth are normally not present at birth. Occasionally, however, a baby will be born with one or more teeth. A tooth in a newborn may be a very early primary (baby) tooth that is anchored in the jaw by a root and should be left alone. If, however, the tooth is "extra" and not firmly rooted into the jaw, it may need to be removed so that it does not pose a choking hazard.

Small white nodules on the gums (Bohn's nodules) or the roof of the mouth (Epstein's pearls) resembling miniature pearls are common, seen in up to eighty percent of newborns. These collections are not worrisome and will disappear over several weeks. Small, firm clear-colored protrusions from the floor of the mouth (ranula) are benign and require no intervention. They are uncommon, seen in less than one percent of newborns.

A newborn's tongue is very active during sucking and will surround the nipple as it draws milk into the mouth. A tongue anchored too tightly to the floor of the mouth will have a notched tip when it is extended and, in rare cases, the "tied" tongue may cause feeding difficulty. In most cases, however, it is not a problem.

Neck

Newborns are born with very weak neck muscles, which cannot support the weight of the head. Occasionally, the muscle on one side of the neck will be tight (torticollis or wryneck), keeping the head tilted toward that side and the face and chin turned and rotated toward the opposite shoulder. A lump may sometimes be noticed within the tight muscle. If you think your baby has a tight neck muscle, please see "torticollis" in the troubleshooting chapter.

Chest

Within your baby's chest, the heart beats normally between 110 and 180 beats per minute and the lungs normally breathe thirty to fifty times per minute. The bony borders of the chest include:

- The breastbone (sternum), which extends from the base of the neck down the center of the chest and ends just above the stomach, in the pointy and sometimes prominent "xiphoid process"

- The "clavicles," which extend from the shoulders to the top of the sternum and are at risk for fracturing during delivery

- The rib cage, wrapping around the chest from the backbone (vertebral column) to the sternum

The chest moves slightly with each breath, and a small dip at the lower portion of the chest may be noticeable with deep breaths inward. A baby normally has two nipples, but additional nipples may be present anywhere between the armpit and the umbilicus. These are variations of normal and have no health concern. Occasionally, a newborn boy or girl has swollen breasts and may even have a small amount of milk draining from the nipples as a result of the mother's hormones. The swelling generally resolves within two years.

The flow of blood through the baby's heart in utero is slightly different from the normal flow of blood through the heart after birth. In utero, a baby's heart has two extra "holes" through which blood flows: the "foramen ovale" allows blood flow through the top two chambers of the heart (the atria), and the "ductus arteriosus" allows blood to flow from the right side of the heart directly to the lower part of the body, bypassing the lungs. After birth, the baby's lungs fill with air and the changes in pressure between the heart and lungs force the holes to close. Blood then follows the normal, adult pattern of flow through the heart. It is not uncommon for an examining pediatrician to hear the noise (murmur) of blood flowing through the holes before they close, soon after birth. Murmurs that persist more than twenty-four hours may require an evaluation by a pediatric cardiologist.

Back

The most important part of your newborn's back is the spinal column, which extends from the nape of the neck down to the buttocks. It is not unusual for newborns to have a very shallow dip, or skin folds in the shape of a V, at the base of the spine. *A deep dimple or a large tuft of hair at the base of the spine may be associated with an abnormality of the underlying spinal cord and should be evaluated by a pediatrician.*

Abdomen

A healthy newborn belly is generally very soft and may be flat or mildly plump. The most noticeable part of your baby's abdomen is the umbilical stump (belly button and cord). The cord was the lifeline during development in utero, carrying blood, oxygen and nutrients between the mother and her growing fetus. Once it is cut and clamped at the time of delivery, your baby must breathe and eat independently of the mother. In the past, it was routine to paint the umbilical stump with a purple liquid to prevent infection, but many hospitals have discontinued that practice. If your baby's cord has not been painted, it will have a light beige/yellow color and you may be able to see three blood vessels within it.

In utero, a baby's intestines develop outside of the abdomen. Eventually, they move into the baby's body at the area of the umbilicus, and a wall of muscles, fibrous tissue, and skin contains them inside the abdomen. In some babies, the abdominal wall muscles separate slightly down the midline, and weakness of the fibrous tissue allows bulging at the umbilicus, especially during crying or straining to pass stool. This "umbilical hernia" may be noticeable throughout most of the first year or longer. Over time, the abdominal wall muscles and the ring of fibrous tissue around the umbilicus strengthen, and the hernia usually disappears. Infrequently, a very large umbilical hernia that persists for several years requires surgical repair. Taping a coin over the bulge is a common practice in some cultures but is not recommended and does not make the hernia disappear any faster.

Genitals

Your baby should have **either** a male penis with a scrotum (sac) **or** a female vagina with labia (folds). *If your baby's genital parts are not distinctly male or female, then your pediatrician may ask a specialist in genetics or endocrinology to evaluate your baby.*

Male (penis and scrotum) – A newborn boy's penis should be at least 2.5 cm (approx. 1 inch) in length. Its tip is covered in a sleeve of skin (foreskin), which is attached to the underlying penis and does not retract easily. If you choose to have your baby circumcised, the foreskin will be removed and you will be able to see the opening at the tip of the penis (urethra). Either way, WATCH OUT—a boy's stream of urine can reach great distances and most caretakers report surprise sprayings. The feeling of cold air on the skin during a diaper change may trigger a spray of urine. The sac beneath the penis is called the scrotum and it contains two testicles. These ball-like structures are the baby's reproductive organs. They are heat sensitive and will hang lower in the sac when the baby is warm, and pull closer to the baby's body when he feels cold. One testicle usually hangs lower than the other. *If you cannot feel both testicles in the sac during a warm bath, a pediatrician should evaluate your baby.* Occasionally, one or both testicles may be surrounded by extra fluid and appear very large. This fluid collection is called a "hydrocele" and usually disappears within the first year.

Female (vagina and labia) – Your baby girl's genitals may appear very dark and swollen after birth and have a large amount of mucous on the inner surfaces. In the skin folds, you will notice some light yellow, soft cheesy material, which is normal and does not need to be removed. Occasionally, a baby girl can bleed from the vagina, as if she is having a period. This bleeding is due to her mother's hormones (remember, they shared a blood supply) and should not last more than a few days.

Arms and legs

Your baby should have two arms, two legs, ten fingers, and ten toes. Newborns keep their arms and legs in a flexed (bent) position, close to their bodies. They should be able to move their left and right sides equally. Occasional abnormalities are noted on the extremities of otherwise healthy babies. Two digits (fingers or toes) may be fused together (syndactyly) or an extra finger or toe may be present (polydactyly). These conditions should be discussed with a pediatrician regarding function, cosmetic concerns, and corrective surgical options.

Newborn legs and feet often appear bowed or curled, a result of the positioning of the baby in the womb. The legs will gradually straighten over the baby's first few years. Arches also develop over several years, but are not well-defined in chubby newborn feet.

Newborn fingernails are very soft. Babies born after their due date tend to have longer fingernails than early or on-time babies, and nails may be stained slightly yellow if a bowel movement was passed in utero prior to delivery.

Skin

Newborn skin goes through many changes throughout the first month of life. In utero, a protective layer of slippery cheese-like cream (vernix caseosa) protects the skin from the liquid environment. The cream washes away easily after birth with soap and water, revealing dry skin that may appear cracked or flaking. The skin color is influenced by the baby's racial group, but many babies have an underlying purplish hue at birth that resolves as the baby's breathing pulls oxygen into its body. For several weeks, the skin color remains variable, turning red with intense crying or becoming "mottled" (marble-like) when exposed to cool air. A yellow tone (jaundice) commonly occurs on the second or third day of life. Aside from the underlying color, several other markings and rashes that commonly occur on newborn skin include:

1. Mongolian spots are dark purple (bruise-like) patches of varying sizes located anywhere on the body but most often on the buttocks, back, legs, and shoulders. These spots are seen on more than ninety percent of babies of east Asian and east African descent, up to fifty percent of Hispanic babies, and less than ten percent of Caucasian babies. They do not affect the health of the baby, and tend to fade away over time.

2. Erythema toxicum is a rash with a scary name but no effect on a baby's health. This rash appears as small (¼ inch) pink patches with raised yellow centers. It typically begins twenty-four to forty-eight hours after birth and may last for several weeks, with old lesions resolving as new ones appear. The rash

may appear anywhere on the body, but the chest is most commonly affected first. Fifty percent of newborns will develop this rash.

3. Pustular melanosis is a rash that occurs anywhere on the body (including the palms and soles) as small raised lesions filled with milky fluid. Within days, the lesions rupture, leaving behind a fine scaly outline. After the scale flakes off, dark spots may persist for several months before fading away completely. In some newborns, the fluid-filled lesions ruptured and flaked while the baby was in utero, and only the dark spots are noticed after delivery. This rash has no effect on the baby's health. Less than five percent of newborns will develop this rash.

4. Nevus simplex markings are commonly known as "stork bites" when they occur on the nape of the neck and "angel kisses" when they occur in the region of the eyebrows and nasal bridge. They are splashes of red coloring that may become more noticeable with crying. They have no effect on the baby's health and usually fade completely over time. More than forty percent of infants will be born with these markings.

5. Milia appear as small white pinpoint bumps on the baby's face, generally around the nose and chin. They have no effect on the baby's health and usually disappear within several weeks. Forty percent of newborns develop milia.

6. Neonatal acne appears as small pimples on a newborn's face within a few weeks after birth. Approximately twenty percent of newborns will

develop acne to varying degrees. These pimples will disappear and should not be popped or treated with acne medication.

7. Hemangiomas are collections of bright red blood vessels that form flat or raised patches. They may appear anywhere on the body and may not be apparent at birth. They often enlarge and become more prominent over the first year of life and then fade away slowly. Most hemangiomas have no effect on the baby's health, but they should be noted and followed by a pediatrician.

8. Bruising and petecchiae (pinpoint red spots that do not blanch when pressed) may result from the trauma of birth. Squeezing pressure as the baby moves through the birth canal causes blood to leak out from the vessels into the surrounding tissue. The same squeezing pressure occurs if the baby's umbilical cord is wrapped tightly around her neck. In that case, the red/purple discoloration occurs most commonly on the face and fades over several days.

9. Café au lait spots are light coffee-colored, oval spots which appear anywhere on the body. A spot may be solitary, or multiple spots may appear at birth or over time. These spots appear more often on African-American newborns (more than fifteen percent) than Hispanic (three percent) or Caucasian newborns (less than one percent). They generally have no clinical significance. If you count more than six large café au lait spots on your baby's skin, you should discuss the finding with your pediatrician.

10. <u>Blue vessels</u> may be noticeable beneath your baby's thin skin, most commonly over the nasal bridge, between the eyes. As your baby develops thicker, deeper skin over the years, the vessels will no longer be noticeable.

11. Beneath the skin, you may be able to feel small nodules or balls, the size of petite peas. These are <u>lymph nodes</u>, which are part of the baby's immune system. Although lymph nodes are scattered throughout the whole body, they are most easily felt in areas where they are closest to the surface. These areas include the back of the neck, behind the ears, the armpits, and the groin where the legs meet the pelvis. Throughout your baby's life, the lymph nodes will enlarge when they are actively fighting infection, and then will shrink back to a small size when their job is done.

Nervous system

The nervous system includes the baby's brain, spinal cord, and the nerves that control the baby's muscles, movements, and sensations. Your baby's "head circumference" (the distance around the widest part of his skull) will be measured at birth and compared to standard head sizes for newborns. Occasionally, "molding" or elongation of the skull will cause the measurement to be small, but as the skull rounds out, the measurement will normalize. Growth of the skull over the first two years will reflect brain growth, and should be checked by your pediatrician at regular checkups. The "spinal cord" runs down the length of the back, protected by the bones of the vertebral column. Obvious abnormalities of the vertebral column, including an opening or very deep dimple of the overlying skin or a tuft of hair, may require further evaluation with ultrasound or X-ray imaging to determine the extent of the abnormality in the spinal cord. Any deficits in function of the muscles may also be related to the nervous system. Babies respond to stimulation by drawing in their arms and legs symmetrically toward their bodies (flexor tone), and floppy tone or asymmetrical movements may require further evaluation of the nervous system. Babies are born with many "reflexes," a few of which are:

Moro (startle) reflex: Lay your baby on his back. Gently pull both arms upward until his shoulders are pulled up slightly off the surface. Quickly let go of both hands, allowing the shoulders to drop back down to the surface. Your baby should suddenly extend and open his arms as if he is making a hugging motion.

Rooting reflex: Stroking your baby's cheek should cause her to turn her head to the stroked side, as if expecting to find a nipple on that side.

Sucking reflex: Your baby will begin to suck on any object placed in his mouth.

Grasp reflex: Applying pressure (or an object) in the palm of your baby's hand causes him to close his fist and grasp the object.

Tonic neck response (fencing reflex): Lay your baby on her back. As you turn her face to one side, the arm and leg on that side should extend outward, while the opposite arm and leg flex.

4
KEEPING BABY SAFE

Transporting

Transporting your newborn home from the hospital may be a nerve-racking experience with every bump and turn. States have laws on child safety seats and some hospitals may not allow your baby to leave the hospital without an approved infant safety seat. The American Academy of Pediatrics has published guidelines on child safety seats based on the child's age, weight, and height. It is recommended that newborns travel in a seat approved for infants, most of which use a five-point harness system in which the straps secure the shoulders, hips, and groin, and originate from the seat itself; the car's seatbelt is then used only to attach the safety seat to the car. All children under twelve years old should ride in the rear seat of the car and infants under one year of age should always face backward. Children should not be placed forward-facing until they are one year old *and* weigh at least twenty pounds. Firm, padded inserts are available for placement in the car seat to prevent the baby's head from moving side to side. The safety seat's straps should fit snugly over the baby's shoulders and may be secured with a snug-fitting breast plate. When properly strapped, not more than one adult finger should fit between the baby's chest and the straps. Many community police departments offer the service of checking infant car seats for proper placement and fit.

The National Highway Traffic Safety Administration can also direct you to a safety seat checkpoint in your area through their Web site (www.nhtsa.dot.gov).

Air travel in modern, pressurized aircrafts is not unsafe for a healthy, full-term newborn. However, the process of air travel, including time spent in crowded airports, unexpected delays, and close, prolonged exposure to other passengers, makes air travel in the newborn period unwise.

* * *

Handling

Newborns are fragile and must be handled gently. Several characteristics of newborns influence their handling recommendations:

Muscle strength and control: Baby muscles may have good *tone*, but they have very little *strength* or *coordination*. Therefore, babies cannot reposition themselves, regain lost balance, or protect themselves. Babies must always be positioned comfortably with no danger of rolling or falling from a surface.

Body proportions: Babies have very large, heavy heads compared to the rest of their bodies. Weak neck muscles are not capable of supporting the head, and so baby heads must always be supported.

Limited ability to communicate: Newborn babies communicate their needs by crying. In addition to feeding and diapering, a newborn needs to feel comfortable and secure. If your baby is crying despite a full tummy, adequate burping, and a dry diaper, consider checking for other sources of discomfort. Straps or bundling that is too tight, restraints that pinch the skin, or rough handling will all cause the baby to cry. With proper adjustments, the baby should be easily soothed.

To properly hold a baby: allow the back of his head to rest within the bend of your elbow. Use the length of your forearm to support the length of his body, and hold his outer hip and upper thigh in your hand. His inner arm (closest to your chest) should be resting gently over his chest and abdomen.

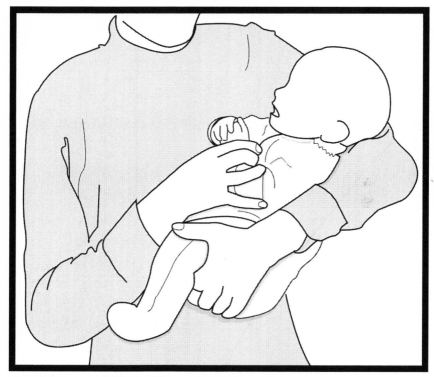

Your baby should be held comfortably, with her head and neck supported.

* * *

Sleep and SIDS (Sudden Infant Death Syndrome)

Newborns spend most of their time sleeping. Current recommendations to keep babies safe during sleep include:

1. Babies should sleep on a firm mattress with tight-fitting sheets. Pillows, blankets, and stuffed toys should **not** be in the baby's sleep space since they pose a hazard of suffocation. Warmth during sleep should come from pajamas or sleeper outfits.

2. Babies should be placed on their **backs** to sleep (not on their bellies or sides).

3. Babies should sleep in a **smoke-free** environment.

4. The room temperature where a baby sleeps should not be above 70°F.

5. A bottle should not be propped into a baby's mouth during sleep.

6. A baby should not be brought into your bed to sleep. Adult beds are generally softer than infant cribs, include looser sheets, blankets, and pillows, and have spaces between the mattress and the bed's frame. Also, you are unconscious during sleep and can easily roll onto and smother or suffocate your baby. Every year, more than sixty children under two years of age are accidentally

smothered or suffocated while sleeping in an adult's bed. Three quarters of those victims are less than three months of age.

* * *

Harmful Foods and Drugs

Breast milk and infant formula are the <u>only</u> substances that should be fed routinely to a baby. Pediatricians may prescribe medications or remedies in specific situations, but in general, caretakers should not be introducing additional foods, drinks, or remedies to newborn babies. Specific substances that may actually be harmful to newborns include:

Honey may be contaminated with spores of *Clostridium botulinum,* a germ that causes infantile botulism. Within the first year of life, an infant infected with botulism may develop progressive weakness, constipation, and severe respiratory difficulty, which may lead to death. Pacifiers should never be dipped in honey (an old-fashioned practice), and baby bottles should not be prepared on surfaces where honey was used.

Maternal medications pass into breast milk to varying degrees. While many substances do not pose a risk to the breast-feeding infant, some have harmful effects and should be avoided by breast-feeding mothers. An obstetrician or pediatrician should be consulted regarding the safety of specific medications during breast-feeding. Taking medications immediately after breast-feeding, when the interval of time until the next feeding is longest, may help to minimize the amount of drug that enters the breast milk. Caffeine, found in coffee, tea, many soft drinks and some pain relievers, will enter breast milk, but many babies are not bothered by a small amount of caffeine in their mother's diet. If a breast-feeding mother includes caffeine in her diet and notices irritability, gassiness, or poor sleeping in her baby, she should consider limiting her caffeine intake.

Recreational drugs and smoking are never healthy and should be avoided. Addictive substances pass through breast milk and are extremely harmful to infants, in addition to compromising a mother's ability to care for her infant with good judgment. <u>Second-hand smoke and smoke residue on clothing</u> is a potent respiratory irritant to children of all ages, but especially to babies who are held frequently and snuggled against the caretaker's body. Alcohol consumption by breast-feeding mothers in *very* limited quantities is probably safe, though never recommended. Maternal alcohol intake can decrease milk production. In addition, alcohol is concentrated in breast milk, and it is recommended to delay breastfeeding for at least two hours after alcohol consumption. Alcohol should *never* be fed directly to an infant for soothing purposes.

Plain water or tea is often given to babies as a remedy for constipation, gassiness or colic. Though the substances themselves do not contain harmful ingredients, they may upset the balance of salt and sugar in a newborn baby and lead to serious complications. A newborn baby has very immature kidneys, which cannot regulate the body's salt balance very well. Excess water will dilute the baby's salt level in the blood, which may lead to seizures. Babies also need a steady supply of sugar until their livers are mature enough to maintain the sugar level in their blood. Breast milk and infant formulas are perfectly balanced in their water, nutrient, and electrolyte content and should be the only substances fed to newborn babies. Commercial rehydration solutions (e.g., Pedialyte, Enfalyte) are water based and include a balance of sugar and electrolytes recommended during vomiting and diarrheal illnesses. They are also a safe alternative to plain water or tea if a caretaker feels that a baby would benefit from a small amount of a water-based drink. They have little nutritional value, though, and should not displace the normal intake of infant formula or breast milk.

* * *

Accessories

Necklaces and long strings that attach pacifiers to a baby's clothing can become twisted or caught and pulled, posing a risk of strangulation. Jewelry such as bracelets, anklets, and rings can potentially cut off circulation to an extremity if placed too tightly, and a loose piece of jewelry that falls off the body may cause choking if it ends up in a baby's mouth. **Any** object small enough to fit in a baby's mouth is considered a choking hazard and should be removed from the vicinity of a baby. Ear piercing is not recommended until six months of age, after the baby has received three doses of tetanus vaccine.

Decorative headbands and hairclips should not be so tight as to leave marks on the skin. If your baby seems irritated by them, they should be removed.

* * *

Pets, siblings, and visitors

Everyone will be very interested in your new baby. Caged pets (hamsters, lizards, birds, fish…) generally pose little risk to babies, as they have no direct access. Free-roaming dogs and cats have their own personalities and their owners must use judgment about how closely they allow their animals to interact with a new baby. A pet dog may be more at ease if your baby's scent is familiar. A receiving blanket or recently worn, unwashed baby outfit can easily transfer your baby's scent from the hospital to your home to prepare your pet ahead of your baby's arrival. However, animals may be unpredictable in their actions and responses, so a good general rule is to keep animals away from new babies. Most importantly, all animals can harbor dangerous germs. Lizards are notorious for carrying salmonella, a diarrheal germ that is deadly to young infants. Birds may be infected with the germ that causes psittacosis, a type of pneumonia that can infect humans. Cats may shed toxoplasmosis germs in their feces that cause a variety of symptoms in humans. *Animal caretakers must always wash their hands thoroughly after handling pets and their cages or litter environments.*

Siblings and visitors also harbor germs. Anyone with a contagious illness should not be around your newborn, and all visitors and siblings should wash their hands prior to handling your baby. Influenza vaccine is recommended for anyone who will have contact with a newborn or infant less than six months old during influenza season. Of course, young children must always be supervised, and never left alone, around newborns.

* * *

Environmental hazards

Newborns, helpless as they are, depend on their caretakers to provide a safe and comfortable environment, inside and outside the home.

Smoke and fire: The air in a baby's environment should always be free of smoke (cigarette, cigar, pipe) and other pollutants. Candles that have lead in their wicks release lead fumes into the air during burning, which can be inhaled and accumulate in the body over time. Candles should be labeled with "lead-free" or "pure cotton" wicks. Candles also expose an open flame, which is a fire hazard. Every home should be equipped with smoke and carbon monoxide detectors. Infants are damaged by much smaller doses of noxious fumes, smoke, and carbon monoxide than adults, and their survival in the event of a fire depends on early warning and evacuation. Any window in their sleeping vicinity should be flagged with a "Tot Finder" decal (available from your local fire department, hardware store, or baby supply store) to alert outside fire and rescue personnel to the location of a dependent child.

Water: Every year, thousands of children are treated in hospital emergency departments for accidental drowning. Approximately fifteen percent of child drowning victims die, and another twenty percent are left with permanent brain damage and disabilities. Of course a newborn cannot wander off to a pool or a pond, but the bathtub is a real hazard. Bathtubs and buckets are the sites of most infant drownings, which occur when an infant is left momentarily unattended or under the supervision of another child. Infants should <u>never</u> be left unattended in a bathtub for any amount of time, under any circumstances! Modern cordless phones make it very convenient to bring the phone within reach to answer during baby's bath. If an activity requires you to leave the side of the bathtub (to answer a doorbell, for example) your baby should be removed from the tub and placed in a safe spot or brought along with you.

Water can also damage a baby when it is too hot. Bath water should be tested with a thermometer (water above 100°F is generally too hot) or your elbow or wrist for comfort prior to contact with baby's skin. If your bath or sink has separate knobs for hot and cold water, always begin and end the bath with the cold-water knob. That is, turn on the cold water first and then add hot water until comfortable water flows from the faucet. End the bath by turning off the hot water first, and then the cold. A splash of cold water may be startling and uncomfortable, but will never burn a baby. Scalding hot water can burn a baby even when it splashes onto skin from a distance.

Sun: Most babies are bothered by direct sun in their eyes and on their skin. Baby skin can easily be sunburned but unfortunately, sunblock lotion is not recommended or approved for infants less than six months old. Wide-brimmed hats and sunglasses, clothing to protect skin, canopies covering strollers, and natural shade from trees and buildings all shield infant eyes and skin from direct sun. Car windows and sunroofs can be tinted or covered with screens to block direct sunlight.

Wind: Most babies do not like direct, forceful wind, though gentle warm breezes may be well tolerated. In addition to discomfort, wind may also cause particles of dust, dirt, or other light objects to fly into a baby's eyes. Babies should be kept inside on <u>very</u> windy days, especially at low temperatures. A wind guard or canopy covering a stroller or infant carrier can protect a baby who must venture outside on a very windy day.

* * *

Infection control

Newborn baby immune systems are very immature and are not good at fighting infections. Therefore, it is extremely important to *prevent* infections and germs from spreading to new babies. Germs are invisible and are found *everywhere* in our environment. Protecting a new baby from infections takes common sense—it is not a good idea to bring a newborn to a crowded mall for holiday shopping, on a crowded city subway, a restaurant, or any other place where many different people deposit their germs. Germs spread by several routes including direct contact, fecal–oral, respiratory droplets, airborne, and through exposure to blood and body fluids.

Direct contact means that germs on a surface (someone's skin, a locker room floor, a towel, etc.) spread to a person only by touching that person. Examples of germs that spread by this route include warts, fungal infections (like ringworm), impetigo (a superficial blistering or crusting skin infection), and herpes, among others. The most effective ways to prevent transmission of these germs is to keep environmental surfaces clean, avoid sharing personal skin items (washcloths, towels, hair brushes), and washing hands frequently since our hands touch dirty environmental surfaces (telephones, doorknobs, etc.) many times daily. Anyone who will be handling your baby should first wash his or her hands, and should not allow an infected skin lesion to contact the baby.

Fecal–oral spread occurs when germs in one person's feces (stool) are "eaten" by another person. When people forget to wash their hands after using the bathroom, fecal germs on their dirty hands spread into food or throughout the environment. The germs are then picked up by others' hands, which may enter their bodies when they touch their mouths or noses, or may contaminate food they prepare. The most common illnesses spread in this manner are the diarrheal infections (viral gastroenteritis, salmonella, shigella, etc.). Summertime colds and rashes also spread by this route. The most important way to prevent spread of these germs is by washing hands after using the bathroom and before preparing or eating food. Newborn babies most often become infected when someone's dirty hands prepare their bottles or handle their pacifiers.

Respiratory droplets include coughs, sneezes, and saliva. Infected respiratory droplets are spewed into the air and settle on environmental surfaces, or are deposited on a person's hand in the process of covering a cough or sneeze and then spread throughout the environment on dirty hands. Another person's hands pick up these germs, which enter their body when they touch their eyes, nose, or mouth. Germs that spread in respiratory droplets cause most common colds, flu, pneumonia and viral rash illnesses, and can also cause more serious infections like meningitis (an infection of the fluid and membranes surrounding the brain and spinal cord). Spread of these germs can be prevented by frequent hand washing, using an inner elbow instead of a hand to cover a cough or sneeze, and throwing away used tissues promptly. Objects that touch the mouth should not be shared, and environmental surfaces should be kept clean. Visitors with coughs or cold symptoms should reschedule their visit or wear a mask over their mouth and nose (available in most drug stores). Baby pacifiers should be cleaned frequently under running water and should not be placed in anyone else's mouth. Infants cannot receive influenza vaccine until six months of age. Therefore, household members and visitors should receive influenza vaccine during influenza season to avoid spreading the infection to your unprotected newborn.

Airborne germs are the most difficult to prevent, but also the least common in the United States. These are germs that are coughed out by an infected person and remain suspended in the air before another person inhales them. Measles and tuberculosis are examples. It is important that babies not be cared for by anyone with an active illness, especially if coughing is a symptom.

Blood and body fluid exposure puts people at risk for contracting illnesses such as HIV, hepatitis B, and hepatitis C, among others. A newborn baby is at risk for these diseases if her mother is infected, which is information that should be determined during pregnancy. Prevention of HIV transmission from a mother to her baby has been very successful with medications given to the mother during pregnancy and delivery, and to the baby after birth. Hepatitis B is preventable by vaccine at the time of birth. There is no preventative treatment for babies born to mothers infected with hepatitis C, but fortunately the infection is not frequently spread through birth.

* * *

CPR (cardio-pulmonary resuscitation)

CPR is a method of restoring blood flow and breathing to a person whose heart and lungs have stopped working. It is a good idea for *everyone* to be trained in CPR, which can save a person suffering from a life-threatening event such as a heart attack, drowning, or choking. All parents and caretakers of infants should also be trained in *infant* CPR. Infants differ from older children and adults in their body size and proportions and the patterns of their respiratory and circulatory systems. Prompt initiation of CPR to an infant who has stopped breathing or appears blue, limp or lifeless can be lifesaving and may preserve brain function and limit future disability. Local hospitals, Red Cross, and American Heart Association (AHA) chapters may offer infant CPR training. The "Infant CPR Anytime" personal learning program, available through the AHA, is a simple, convenient, and inexpensive way for a family to learn infant CPR in the privacy of their own home. The kit can be ordered through the AHA Web site or by calling 1-877-AHA-4CPR.

* * *

Child abuse

Actions that lead to devastating outcomes for babies and their parents include:

Shaking: It is *never* OK to shake a baby with vigor or force. Persistent crying is the reason most babies are shaken forcefully by caretakers. There is no doubt that loud, constant crying can infuriate and aggravate a tired, sleep-deprived caretaker. However, shaking a baby only stops the crying by causing brain damage. *Shaking a baby is a serious form of child abuse.* It causes shaken baby syndrome, which damages babies' brains, eyes, and bodies. It is a crime punishable by imprisonment and ruins lives and families. Any person in any social situation from poverty to luxury is capable of committing this crime.

If you ever feel angry with your baby or believe you may strike or shake your baby:

> 1. Place your baby somewhere safe, such as in a crib or bassinet, and take a break. Earplugs will dull any loud crying, and music may draw your focus away from the stress of baby care.

2. Call someone nearby (a relative or neighbor) to help you manage the baby while you take a break or a much-needed nap.

3. Call a local hospital emergency room or police department to inquire about any local crisis hotline or crisis-intervention services available in your area. Or, call the Childhelp hotline at 1-800-4Achild (1-800-422-4453). Childhelp is a national organization that offers immediate crisis counseling. They also refer callers to local parenting and child safety resources listed in their national database. It is never a crime to reach out for help.

Leaving your baby unattended: Babies are dependent on their caretakers for <u>everything</u>—feeding, bathing, diapering, protection from harm, and rescue from accidents or dangerous situations. Leaving a baby unattended may have disastrous consequences if an unfortunate accident were to occur. An example: your baby is sleeping in his crib and you go out to the store for a few grocery items. While you are out, a fire starts in your home or apartment; or your baby has a seizure; or you have a car accident and are taken unconscious to a local ER. In each situation, the baby is in grave danger and would have a much better outcome if a caretaker were available to respond to the situation. It is very poor judgment and a child abuse crime to leave a baby unattended.

5
NEWBORN FUNCTIONS

Eating and growing

Newborns should be eager to eat and suck vigorously on a nipple at frequent intervals of one and a half to three hours. Signs of hunger in a newborn include increased movement, alertness, mouthing, and rooting motions. Crying is a late sign of hunger. It is always best to offer milk at the first signs of hunger, so that the pace of the feeding is enthusiastic, not frantic. Feeding a baby on demand in response to early cues also helps to develop a sense of trust. Generally, feeding intervals should not exceed four hours, and a newborn should be woken to feed if the interval is nearing four hours. Feeding difficulties such as lack of interest, choking on feeds, breathing difficulty during feeds, discomfort, excessive spilling of milk out of the lips, and vomiting should be evaluated by a pediatrician.

All the eating leads to growing, and a well-fed baby should grow steadily. At birth, babies are slightly swollen with fluid. Within their first few days, they shed the extra fluid and may normally lose five to ten percent of their birth weight. By seven to ten days, they should regain or surpass their birth weight, and should continue to gain approximately an ounce each day through the rest of their first month. Growth spurts occur throughout the first year, when increases in feeding and sleeping are noticeable, resulting in a sudden increase in the baby's weight. Growth spurts in infancy usually occur around three weeks, six weeks, three months, six months, and nine months of age.

* * *

Burping

Air enters our gastrointestinal tracts every time we swallow. Babies feed frequently, and therefore swallow frequently, and tend to accumulate large collections of gas in their stomachs. Fortunately, air rises out of liquids, so that if a baby's head is in a position higher than the stomach, gas bubbles escape from the body through the mouth as a burp. Gas that is not released as a burp will travel the entire length of the intestinal tract and exit through the anus. Gas bubbles traveling through the intestine may cause discomfort, so it is a good idea to encourage burping at the time of feeding.

Many babies burp on their own when their head is positioned higher than their stomach. This can be accomplished by three different positions (see figure):

1. Rest the baby's chest and belly against your shoulder and chest.

2. Place him on his stomach.

3. Place him in a forward sitting position with your hand supporting his lower jaw and chin (be careful not to press on his neck).

Gentle tapping on his back in any of these positions will mobilize the bubbles and encourage them to rise.

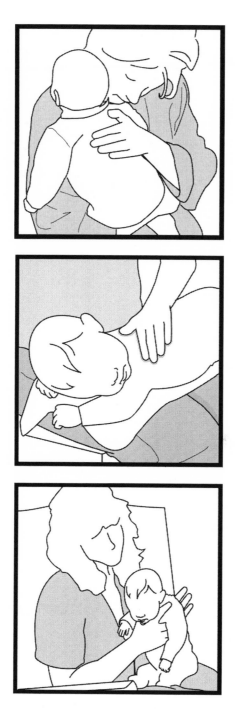

Place your baby over your chest and shoulders, lying across your lap face down, or in a sitting position on your lap. These positions allow gas to rise from the stomach to the mouth to be expelled.

53

Some babies do not burp well, in which case the swallowed air eventually passes through the anus. To minimize gas intake, make sure your baby's lips have a good seal around the widest part of the nipple. A poor seal will allow gas to enter past the loose lips as the baby sucks in the nipple, and the feeding will be noisy. Also, if your baby is bottle-feeding, always make sure the nipple is held at an angle so its tip is filled with milk, not air.

Additional gas is produced further within the intestinal tract by bacteria that aid in digestion. This gas is too far from the stomach to be released in a burp, and will be passed through the anus. Therefore, no matter how well your baby burps, flatus (farts) is inevitable.

* * *

Sleeping

Sleep is one of the most important functions of your newborn baby as it grows rapidly and recovers from the trauma of birth. Most newborns will sleep for two- to three-hour periods throughout the day and night, waking for feedings. In a twenty-four-hour period, a typical healthy newborn spends a total of approximately fourteen to eighteen hours sleeping. Unfortunately, many of the wakeful hours occur in the wee hours of the night, a pattern that may persist for several weeks or months. Some babies prefer to be held at sleep time, rather than lie alone in a crib or cradle. Allowing a baby to sleep in your arms is fine, as long as you remain awake. If you fall asleep with the baby in your arms, your baby is at risk for rolling, falling, or being smothered.

Over time, babies begin to spend more hours awake and alert, interacting and becoming familiar with their environment. Spending time outside in fresh air and sunshine (on a nice day, and properly dressed) is stimulating, and has a positive effect on the establishment of a healthy sleep schedule. It is also helpful to adhere to a routine around bedtime, which may include a warm bath, a breast or bottle feeding with burping, dim lighting, a favorite song or story, and placement in the crib or bassinet in a quiet, drowsy state. Babies feel secure with routines, and the anticipation of sleep as a step in an established routine has a great sedative effect.

* * *

Crying

Crying is your baby's only way to communicate her needs—for food, comfort, soothing, or sleep. It is generally very unpleasant to hear a baby crying, which is nature's way of motivating a caretaker to remain attentive and responsive to a baby's needs. Occasionally, a caretaker may hear the baby crying, only to find the baby sleeping or resting quietly. These "phantom cries" usually occur when there is background noise, and may be another of nature's ploys to ensure that the baby is checked frequently. Some caretakers can distinguish the baby's need based on subtle differences in the cry quality. When a newborn cries, the reason should be sought. If she has been fed, burped and diapered, persistent crying may indicate discomfort from a diaper rash, fever, tight clothing and bundling, or a need for comfort and soothing or sleep. Keep in mind that a newborn's responses, including crying, are mostly reflexive and innate. Therefore, a newborn's preference to be held and rocked is a *need*, which develops her sense of trust and leads to a healthy relationship with caretakers. Holding a newborn when she cries will not spoil her. If, despite *all* needs being met, your baby remains inconsolable, you should consult your pediatrician.

* * *

Eliminating Waste

Wetting and soiling diapers with urine and stool are very necessary functions. These functions are not voluntary. A baby's bladder will release its urine when it fills to a certain volume, and the rectum is activated whenever a feeding stimulates the stomach. After the first few days of life, the bladder generally empties urine six or more times per day (twenty-four-hour period). Modern diapers are extremely absorbent, though, and need not be changed after each urine void. The urine should be clear or yellow, and occasional orange or pink stains may be noticed in the lining of a newborn's diaper overlying the urine spot. These are caused by crystals formed in the kidney and should resolve once the baby begins feeding well and passing plenty of urine.

Stool output is variable. The earliest stool (called meconium) is black and sticky like tar and should be passed within twenty-four hours after birth. After a few days, the stool gradually turns green, brown, or yellow, often described as "mustard" color and may appear to be filled with sesame seeds (particularly in breast-fed babies). Stooling patterns are variable for both breast- and formula-fed babies. Some babies have a bowel movement after each feed or at least several times each day, while others may have one only every other day or every few days. Whatever your baby's pattern, the stool that passes should be soft (mushy or pasty) with plenty of color (in the autumn palette—yellow, green, or brown). If your baby's skin is yellow (a condition called jaundice), his stool should also be very yellow as it eliminates the bilirubin (the substance responsible for the yellow skin color) from the baby's body.

Situations that warrant a call to your baby's pediatrician include:

1. Multiple orange or pink stains appear in the lining of the diaper in a twenty-four-hour period, especially if your baby is breast-fed.

2. By the third day of life your baby is not passing urine regularly, at least once in each six- to eight-hour period. By the fifth day, your baby should void at least five times each day.

3. Your baby's urine has a strong or unpleasant odor or is dark in color.

4. Your baby's stool is white or clay colored.

5. Your baby's stool is hard like rocks or pellets or has blood on its surface.

6. Infrequent stools are accompanied by vomiting, distension (bloating) of the abdomen or refusal to feed.

7. Your baby's stool is watery, extremely foul smelling, or contains blood.

* * *

Bonding and attachment

Bonding is the positive emotional connection that a caretaker feels for her baby. Likewise, a baby develops a similar sense of attachment to a familiar and attentive caretaker. Strong bonds and attachments take time to develop, but newborns begin to use their five senses to develop their emotional connection right from birth:

1. Sight - Newborns prefer to look at a human face more so than any other form. During feeds, an alert baby cradled in a person's arm may gaze up to look at the feeder's face. *If your baby does not regard your face with interest and you are concerned about her ability to see, consult your pediatrician.*

2. Sound - Newborns are soothed by high-pitched female voice tones and are comforted by sounds and voices familiar to them. Speaking or singing during routines activities (diaper changes, baths, sleeping) may be tremendously comforting to a newborn. *If you believe your baby does not respond to sound, consult your pediatrician. Even a baby who has passed the newborn hearing test can have a hearing impairment.*

3. Smell - A baby has a very strong sense of smell, which is especially keen for his mother's milk and human body scent.

4. Taste – Babies prefer sweet flavors and can detect subtle differences among varieties of infant milk. A baby bonded to breast-feeding can distinguish his mother's milk from all other milks and may prefer the taste and smell of her nipple and milk to any substitute.

5. Touch – Newborns love to be held, and some may cry and fuss nonstop unless they are being held by a person. It is especially soothing to a newborn to be held on a person's chest where body warmth and a rhythmic heartbeat can be felt.

Gentle infant massage combines several sensations to reinforce feelings of bonding and attachment. The *sight* of a human face, the *sound* of a soft voice, the *scent* of natural plant oils and the *touch* of warm hands rubbing an infant's skin and muscles from head to toe all combine to provide a very positive experience for a baby and her caretaker. Books and DVD's on the topic of infant massage are available, and many local hospitals or community-based parenting education resources can refer caretakers to certified infant massage instructors.

6
CLEANING AND GROOMING

Soaps, shampoos, detergents, and bathing

Newborn skin is very sensitive. Chemicals that add color or fragrance to creams, lotions, soaps, and detergents may be irritating, and some textures (such as wool or fabric containing metallic thread) may also be uncomfortable. Your baby should always be handled in clothing or blankets made of fabric that is nonirritating, such as cotton. All new articles of clothing, towels, washcloths, burp cloths, and bedding should be laundered in a gentle, hypoallergenic detergent before use.

Soaps and shampoos should be used infrequently, as they tend to strip the skin of natural oils. Since newborn activities generally do not include sandboxes or mud pies, dirt is generally not a big concern for newborn hygiene. However, newborns do shed many layers of skin and soil their diapers regularly. Therefore, bathing two to three times per week with a mild soap, shampoo, or body wash helps to avoid an accumulation of grime, dead skin cells, and germs. Soaps and shampoos used on newborn skin should be labeled "hypoallergenic" and "no tears" to minimize skin and eye irritation.

Sponge bathing is the recommended method of cleaning the newborn baby for the first few weeks of life. Newborns generally are not "dirty" outside of their diaper areas, which should be cleaned well during diaper changes, and do not need to be bathed more than two or three times each week. In fact, excessive bathing with soap will remove the protective natural oils from your baby's skin, causing dryness and discomfort. Many newborns do not even enjoy bath time, as the air feels cold over their wet skin.

Sponge bathing uses a clean washcloth with a very small amount of warm soapy water to cleanse each body part individually, followed by a fresh, warm water rinse. This is the most practical method of cleaning a newborn for several reasons: first, it allows the umbilical cord to remain dry, which promotes separation from the body; second, it limits the baby's exposure to cool air during bath time; and lastly, it is safer than bathing a slippery baby in a tub of water. To sponge bathe a newborn, follow these steps:

First, choose a location:

Kitchen or bathroom countertop: These sites are conveniently located near a sink where water is readily available and its temperature is easily adjusted. The height is generally comfortable for the caretaker but babies placed on countertops must be carefully handled and constantly supervised to prevent falls over the edge. A waterproof mattress pad underlying a thick bath towel is comfortable for the baby and prevents large puddles.

Crib or changing table: The crib is a safe place to sponge-bathe a baby. Side rails protect against falls over the edge, and the mattress provides a comfortable surface. A waterproof pad should be used to protect the mattress.

Bathtub or sink: A bathtub or large sink has the advantage of a nearby source of water and a surface that does not require protection from water spills. A portable baby bathtub with a drain plug can be used within the full-size tub, or a cushioned nonslip pad can be placed beneath the baby for comfort and to prevent slipping. Hazards in sinks and tubs include hot water splashing onto the baby from a running faucet and rapid accumulation of water that may occur if the drain is blocked or the water flow is heavy.

Floor: If no other site is available to you, consider the floor. This is the safest location to sponge bathe a baby since a slippery baby would have nowhere to fall. The floor should be clean and situated away from high-traffic or drafty areas. A waterproof mattress pad underlying a thick bath towel is comfortable for the baby and protects the floor from water damage. Floor bathing requires the caretaker to sit, kneel, or bend, which may be uncomfortable.

After deciding on the bath location, gather your supplies: two soft, clean baby washcloths, two small basins filled with clean warm* water (only one if you will be nearby running water), mild soap (liquid cleanser labeled for use on babies is ideal), baby moisturizer (optional), bath towels and a waterproof pad.

*Baby skin is very thin and can be easily burned by hot water. Generally, water above 100°F is uncomfortably *hot on a baby's skin. You should check the water with a thermometer or your wrist or elbow for comfort before bathing your baby.*

Begin by placing your clothed baby on a thick bath towel overlying a waterproof pad if you are on a surface other than a bathtub or sink. Position him so that he is lying on his back with his feet closest to you. Add a very small amount of soap or cleanser to one basin to make a dilute cleansing solution with few bubbles.

The bath should progress from head to toe:

The baby's face should be wiped with the fresh water washcloth only and no soaps, creams, or lotions should be applied. The second washcloth should be saturated with the mild soapy solution and then squeezed out so that it is not dripping wet. Use this second washcloth to wash the hair, neck, ear folds, and the skin behind the ears with the mild soap solution. No attempt should be made to clean the ear canals, but if water or mild cleanser enters the canals, it is not harmful. Vernix caseosa, the cheesy material that covers newborn skin at birth, fills the ear canals initially, and is soon replaced by a protective layer of wax. At the end of the ear canal, the ear drum prevents water from damaging the delicate structures of the middle ear.

After cleansing, the soap should be rinsed thoroughly from the head, neck, and ears by squeezing water from the fresh water washcloth so that water drips onto the skin and flows toward the back of the head.

Remove the clothing from the baby's upper body (arms, shoulders, back, chest, and belly). Use the mildly soapy washcloth to cleanse the exposed skin. Again, squeeze water from the fresh water cloth to rinse the soap from the skin. If your baby's umbilical cord remains attached, do your best to keep it dry by bathing around it. If you'd like to use moisturizer, apply it to damp skin at this time. Powders are not recommended because the particles may be inhaled or may settle in the baby's eyes. Once the upper body has been cleaned, cover it with a dry towel and bathe the lower body (diaper area, hips, legs, and feet) the same way. Again, apply moisturizer to wet skin if desired. At the end of the bath, you may want to squeeze some fresh water down your baby's backside if he has been lying on a wet, soapy towel. Once your baby has been rinsed completely, apply moisturizer to his back if desired, and transfer him to a clean, warm towel. Re-dress him in clean clothing and brush his scalp with a very soft baby brush or comb to remove any loose, dead skin cells.

WARNING: It is very common for babies to pass urine when they feel cool air on their skin. Be careful with boys, especially, that you are not in the path of the urine stream.

Tub bathing can replace sponge bathing after the umbilical cord separates. However, it is also fine to continue sponge bathing your baby for as long as you'd like.

Generally, tub baths take place in a sink or tub, and commercial portable baby bathtubs are available to be placed in the full-size tub. Wherever you bathe your baby, there should be a drain to allow rapid drainage of bath water and a mat or cushion should line the bottom surface to prevent sliding. Tub bathing differs from sponge bathing in that the baby is fully undressed for the duration of the bath. The baby should lie at an inclined angle of approximately 45° so that the head and shoulders are elevated, and the water should not be more than two to three inches deep. Mild skin cleanser can be mixed directly into the shallow bath water and the baby's entire body and scalp can be cleaned quickly. Clear running tap water at a comfortable temperature (95–100°F) can then be used to wash the face and rinse the body after the soapy water is drained. A shower hose attached to the tub faucet, a standard sprayer in a kitchen sink, or a small pitcher is useful during the fresh water rinse.

* * *

Cord care

Umbilical cords are made of live tissue and blood vessels. Cutting and clamping the cord at birth causes the tissue to die. As the dead tissue dries, it becomes dark and shriveled and falls off the body. This process generally occurs within seven to ten days but may take several weeks. During that time, umbilical cords require very little care. In fact, even with no special attention, the cord will fall off just in the course of nature. However, the stump becomes unsightly over time and bacteria that feed on dead skin may produce an unpleasant odor. Occasionally bacteria infect the surrounding skin, causing redness and inflammation. For these reasons, "cord care" involves:

1. Keeping the cord dry: While the cord is attached, the baby should be sponge bathed so that the flow of bath water can be controlled to avoid the cord.

The diaper edge can be folded down so that the cord is exposed to air beneath the clothing, which promotes drying. Newborn diapers are available with a notch in the upper edge that exposes the cord.

2. Swabbing the umbilical stump with isopropyl (rubbing) alcohol is an effective way of reducing the number of bacteria on the stump and promoting drying. The alcohol should be applied around the entire base of the stump where the dead cord tissue meets the healthy inner skin of the future belly button. Light pressure on the stump in different directions helps to expose the deep surfaces to be swabbed. A Q-tip dipped in rubbing alcohol can then easily reach into the skin folds and crevices around the base of the umbilicus.

3. As the cord falls off, a small amount of blood may be noticeable on the overlying clothing or diaper edge and is not cause for concern. After the cord falls off, the base of the belly button should be flesh-colored and dry. A moist yellow or pink surface indicates incomplete healing of the skin. Your pediatrician can decide if it requires additional cleaning or further topical treatment.

* * *

Circumcision care

"Circumcision" is the surgical removal of the foreskin, which is the sleeve of skin surrounding the tip of the penis. It is an optional procedure, and the decision to circumcise a boy is often influenced by cultural tradition or personal preference. The only recognized medical benefit of circumcision is a lower rate of urinary tract infections in the first year of life, and protection against penile cancer, which is rare, in later life. In general, the circumcision is performed during the nursery stay, although it may be done later at other sites including obstetrician, pediatrician, or urologist offices or home religious ceremonies.

During the procedure, most of the foreskin is cut and removed. The tip of the penis may be covered by Vaseline-impregnated gauze, which loosens as urine passes through it, and generally falls off within twenty-four to forty-eight hours. If the gauze dressing remains beyond two days, drops of warm water will help to loosen it, easing its removal. The tip of the circumcised penis is initially beefy red. There may be some swelling at the site where the foreskin was cut. With each diaper change, a dab of lubricant (petroleum jelly, A+D ointment, or bacitracin, an antibacterial ointment) should be applied to the penis and the front of the diaper to prevent the raw skin of the penis from sticking to the diaper.

As the penis heals, a wet, yellow coating resembling pus will form. This is the normal appearance of the healing penis, and the yellow coating will slough off within a week. During the healing phase, you should contact your baby's pediatrician if:

1. The circumcision site bleeds excessively, evident by blood soaking into the diaper.

2. Your baby does not pass urine within twelve hours after circumcision.

3. Your baby develops a fever (rectal temperature 100.4°F or more).

4. Swelling and redness extend from the circumcision site toward the baby's belly.

Once the circumcision site heals, it is important to prevent what is left of the foreskin from reattaching to the glans (tip) of the penis. Baby boys develop a "fat pad" on the lower abdomen just above the area where the penis originates. This fat pad tends to push the remaining foreskin forward toward the tip of the penis. Body oils and creams accumulate over time between the leftover foreskin and the tip of the penis, and "glue" the foreskin back down to the glans. Consequently, the rim of the head of the penis becomes obscured (see figure). Although the penis still functions properly, the reattached foreskin may lead to future discomfort when forceful erections pull the two adherent skin surfaces apart rapidly, leaving a raw, sore spot. Adhesions can be prevented by simply cleaning beneath the rim of the head of the penis with each diaper change. Gently sliding the remaining foreskin back toward the body will expose the rim and allow for easy cleaning.

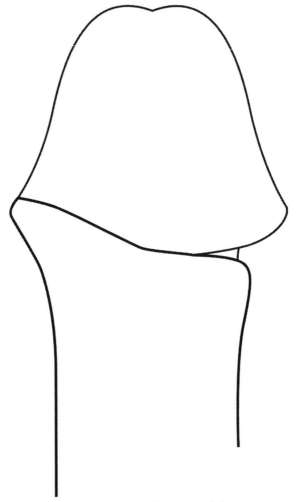

Penile adhesion: To prevent reattachment of the circumcised foreskin, be sure to clean beneath the rim.

Care of the uncircumcised penis

An uncircumcised penis has a foreskin attached to the head of the penis, surrounding it like a sleeve. It covers the urethral opening at the tip of the penis, through which urine flows, but is generally not obstructive to the flow of urine. There is no reason to try to retract the foreskin from the head of the penis, and doing so may lead to great discomfort for the baby. If a forcibly retracted foreskin is then not replaced, dangerous restriction of blood flow may occur, causing damage to the penis. Over several years, your baby will have erections that will slowly detach and stretch the foreskin and allow it to retract easily. Until then, the foreskin should be left undisturbed and cleaned like any other skin during diaper changes and baths.

Care of the female genital area

Newborn girls normally have sticky, cheesy material within the folds of their labia. This material is difficult to remove and should be left in place. Eventually, it will loosen and fall away from your baby's skin. The only care that female genital parts require is gentle surface wiping during diaper changes, directing stool away from the vagina and labia, back toward the anus. Stool is full of germs and can cause irritation or infection when it contaminates areas outside of the gastrointestinal tract.

After several months, the estrogen hormone that passed from the mother's blood to her infant wears off. Lacking the lubricant effect of estrogen, girls' inner labia (labia minora) may become partially adherent, or stuck together, following minor irritation. When this occurs, the labia usually join or fuse together at their lower edges, while the frequent flow of urine prevents fusion at their top edges. Without treatment, the labia will separate naturally due to hormones and changes in the vaginal fluid during adolescence. Your pediatrician may recommend a topical hormone cream during infancy if your baby's labia are almost completely fused, obstructing the flow of urine, or if irritation or infection develops from trapped urine or stool beneath the fused edges.

71

* * *

Diapering

Changing diapers is one of the most repetitive tasks in infant care and requires very little explanation. You will have many opportunities to practice and will quickly develop expertise. The following points should be kept in mind:

Cloth vs. Disposable

The decision to use cloth diapers or disposable diapers is a personal preference, largely influenced by lifestyle and environmental conscience. <u>Cloth diapers</u> require more frequent changes since the baby's waste remains in contact with the skin surface. They also require laundering since they are reusable. They are less costly (because they are reusable) but their cost may be driven up if you contract with a diaper service that provides laundering and delivery of fresh diapers. <u>Disposable diapers</u> are much more convenient and readily available but they do account for a large volume of garbage that does not decompose readily. There are many brands to choose from at a variety of prices, textures, and scents. They do not require changing after every wetting since the urine is absorbed into the deep gel layers of the diaper and removed from contact with the skin.

Diaper Placement

Disposable diapers have one end with adhesive tabs and the other end with a decorative strip across the top. When a fresh diaper is opened, the end with the adhesive tabs should be placed beneath the baby's back. The other end is then folded up to cover the baby's front genitals, and the decorative strip will lie across the baby's lower abdomen. The adhesive tabs are then pulled from behind to connect the back of the diaper to the front. Boys' penises should always be pointed downward toward their legs before the diaper is secured. If not, the stream of urine is directed to the front or side edges at the waistband, and may leak upward toward the abdomen or back.

When changing a soiled diaper, detach the adherent tabs from the front decorative strip to open the diaper. Lift your baby's legs to expose the genital area and wipe your baby from <u>front to back</u>, pushing stool away from the urinary tract. Leave the dirty wipe(s) inside the diaper and remove the entire diaper from his body, pressing the diaper closed to contain the dirty wipes and stool. Fold and roll the bottom of the dirty diaper up toward its decorative strip. Wrap the adhesive tabs tightly around the bundle of dirty diaper and wipes, containing the mess. Place a fresh diaper on your baby, then dispose of the dirty bundle and wash your hands.

Most diapers are sized by number, and most packages will provide a weight range for proper fit. Though "newborn" size diapers are available, it is not advisable to buy too many, as babies quickly outgrow that first size. National brands are, of course, much more expensive than store brands. You will have plenty of opportunity to try different brands to find your favorite.

Wipes, Creams, Ointments, and Powder

There are as many brands and varieties of wipes as there are of diapers. Wipes are extremely convenient. They are premoistened, which allows for easier, more comfortable removal of urine and stool from the sensitive diaper area, and are available with a variety of pleasant scents and moisturizers or skin conditioners. They are packaged in convenient plastic tubs that can be replenished frequently with refill packs. They also are available in travel cases that fit conveniently into diaper bags. They can be used to wipe skin anywhere on the body as the need arises. If your baby's skin is irritated by wipes, consider rinsing the wipe with warm water to remove the scents and preservatives before use. Remember that wipes should never be flushed down a toilet! They should be disposed of along with the dirty diaper in an appropriate trash container.

Creams for the diaper area are generally ointment based (e.g., petroleum jelly, A+D ointment) or zinc oxide based (e.g., Desitin, Balmex). Both protect the skin by creating a barrier layer between the skin of the diaper area and the urine and stool. It is not necessary to use creams or ointments on healthy skin, but you may find that your baby develops fewer diaper rashes if the skin is protected. Once a rash develops, these products can help the skin to heal by protecting it from ongoing contact with urine or stool. Generally, the zinc oxide creams are more effective than ointments for healing an established rash. If your baby develops a diaper rash that does not improve with use of over-the-counter creams or ointments, you should consult your pediatrician. Babies can have diaper rashes infected with yeast or bacteria, which require medicated creams.

Use of powders in the diaper area or elsewhere is discouraged. Powders were a popular way to absorb surface moisture and reduce friction when cloth diapers were commonly used. Now, disposable diapers draw the wetness into an inner gel layer, out of direct contact with the skin. Also, powders can aerosolize and the particles can be inhaled or settle into a baby's eyes.

* * *

Hair, Scalp, and Skin Care

Babies are born with a variable amount of hair. Newborn hair requires very little care. Gentle cleansing with a mild head and body cleanser during bath time two to three times per week is adequate. The scalp (including the area over the soft spot) should be brushed regularly after bathing or more frequently to remove loose skin cells. Dead skin cells can become trapped beneath the hair and form a layer of scales on the scalp. Seborrheic dermatitis is common in newborns and can also cause a thick crust of greasy, yellow scales to accumulate on your baby's scalp ("cradle cap"), face, ears, neck, and diaper area. If scales develop on your baby's scalp, they are easy to remove. Simply rub some baby oil or petroleum jelly (which is not as drippy) into the area of scales. Allow it to sit for ten to twenty minutes, and then shampoo your baby's scalp. Comb your baby's scalp backward with a soft baby brush or comb, and the scales should lift up easily. You may have to repeat this procedure over several days, depending on the thickness or extent of the scaling. Occasionally, babies with seborrheic dermatitis require medicated shampoos for very extensive or thick-crusted scales on their scalp. If you are unable to remove your baby's scales, your pediatrician can decide if a medicated shampoo is necessary.

At birth, newborns are covered in a layer of cheesy material called "vernix caseosa," which protects their skin from the liquid environment in utero. After this layer is easily washed off, the skin will normally flake and peel down to a fresh layer of healthy newborn skin. It is not necessary to put any moisturizers or creams on the skin while it is flaking and peeling. After you begin bathing the baby regularly, you may want to apply a layer of hypoallergenic moisturizer on wet skin after each bath to replace the moisture and natural oils removed by the skin cleanser. This becomes more important in cold, dry environments when winter air and indoor heating cause additional moisture to evaporate from the skin.

* * *

Clipping Nails

Newborn nails are very soft, but harden over time. Babies born past their due dates tend to have longer nails, and distressed babies who pass stool in utero may have finger nails that are slightly discolored. Fingernails grow much more quickly than toenails and must be trimmed frequently to avoid accidental scratching of the face and eyes. Trimming finger and toenails is best accomplished with a baby-sized nail clipper, blunt-tipped nail scissor, or nail file. A nail file is preferred, as it allows rounding of the corners and poses little risk of accidentally cutting skin. A nail clipper or scissor is a faster method, but may leave sharp corners and risks cutting skin and causing bleeding. If you choose to use a clipper or scissor, gently roll the fingertip back, moving the skin away from the nail. Clip the center of the nail straight across, and allow a small band of nail to remain beyond the fingertip. If the corners of the nail are left pointy, reposition the clipper or scissor to trim each corner, but avoid digging into the sides of the fingertip.

Trimming nails by either method is easiest while the baby is sleeping and the hand is relaxed. A baby who is awake is unlikely to cooperate and will tend to move and close his hands in a fist position. Remember that your baby is born with a grasp reflex, which causes him to make a tight fist around anything that touches his palm. Lifting and separating each finger by its top surface, without touching the palm or underside of the fingers, may avoid triggering the grasp reflex. If you find yourself getting frustrated before all ten nails are trimmed, it is best to take a break and finish the remaining nails another time.

* * *

Q-tips

Q-tips have only two uses in newborn care. First, a Q-tip dipped in isopropyl (rubbing) alcohol is the best tool for cleaning and drying an umbilical cord. As the cord is gently pulled upward or pushed to the side, an alcohol-soaked Q-tip can swab around the entire base of the cord where it attaches to the abdomen. Q-tips can reach into crevices and their cotton fibers pick up old scabs and dirt particles. The second use for Q-tips is to clean the outer ears. A Q-tip with some baby oil or petroleum jelly can reach into the tight folded cartilage and pull out shed skin cells or trapped dirt. It is <u>not</u> recommended to push a Q-tip into the ear canal (the hole leading into the head) since doing so just pushes wax and debris farther into the canal and risks damaging delicate structures. Ear canals are also very sensitive and it may not be a comfortable feeling for the baby.

7
KEEPING BABY HEALTHY

Breast- and formula feeding

Babies are born with a "sucking" reflex and will suck on anything placed in their mouth. They are also born with a "rooting" reflex and will open their mouths and turn their heads to the side when their cheek is stroked, expecting to find a nipple. They are born eaters. Their most natural food is human breast milk, which is complete nutrition, containing a balance of protein (whey and casein), carbohydrate (lactose), and fats (cholesterol, triglycerides, and fatty acids). An alternative to breast milk is infant formula, which is regulated by the Food and Drug Administration (FDA) and is required to meet nutritional standards for infants through the first year.

Breast or bottle...

The decision to feed your baby breast milk or commercial infant formula (or both) is often based on personal preference. Human milk is recommended as the best and most appropriate milk for infants, but there are a few situations where breast milk or breast-feeding may be harmful and is discouraged. These include:

HIV infection in the mother – Dramatic decreases in the transmission of HIV infection from an infected mother to her baby during birth have been accomplished by the use of anti-HIV medications during pregnancy,

79

delivery, and in the weeks after birth. However, the HIV virus can still be transmitted through breast milk.

Untreated tuberculosis in the mother – Tuberculosis can be transmitted through the breast milk when it causes mastitis or a breast abscess. More often, the infection passes from mother to baby through close contact with respiratory secretions. If tuberculosis disease is suspected in a mother, she and her infant should be temporarily separated until her disease status is evaluated. Medication may be required for both mother and baby, and any other infected close contacts. Infants who contract this infection are at great risk for overwhelming, complicated disease including meningitis, which may cause permanent brain damage.

Breast abscess (pus-filled infection) involving the milk ducts – The pus of an abscess is packed with bacteria. If an abscess on a woman's breast involves the milk ducts, large loads of bacteria will spill into the milk. Milk expressed from the affected breast should be discarded until the infection is adequately treated. It is fine, however, to continue breast-feeding from the unaffected breast. Many women develop "mastitis," an inflammatory condition caused by blockage of the ducts with backed-up milk. Mastitis may become infected, but will resolve more quickly if the baby sucks frequently at the breast to restore free flow of the milk and relieve the blocked ducts.

Herpes or syphilis lesions on the nipple – A baby should not be fed through a nipple that has visible herpes or syphilis lesions. Feeding from the other breast can continue if its nipple is free of infection. Milk expressed through the infected nipple should be discarded, and then feeding from both breasts can resume after the lesions heal completely.

Certain medications that pass into breast milk – Not all medications that a woman takes pass into breast milk, and not all medications that do pass into breast milk are harmful. If you plan to breast-feed, you should discuss the safety of any medications you are taking with your doctor. If you need to begin any new medications while you are breast-feeding, remind the prescribing physician that you are breast-feeding. If the medication that you need is not safe during breast-feeding, consider pumping and discarding your breast milk during the time you are taking the medication. By maintaining your flow of milk, you will be able to resume breast-feeding once the medication is discontinued.

Certain diseases in the newborn that require a restricted diet – Unfortunately, some babies are born with abnormalities in the chemistry of their bodies. Every state in our country has a "newborn screening" program that tests all newborns at birth for some of these abnormalities. Some babies are discovered to have abnormalities not included in the newborn screen after they develop symptoms over time. If your baby is found to have an abnormality in the chemistry or an organ system of his body, he may require a very specialized infant formula to keep his body healthy and in balance.

If you and your baby have none of the conditions listed above, you should go ahead and breast-feed if that is your desire. If, for any reason, you would prefer to feed your baby infant formula, that is fine too. Many mothers choose to feed both breast milk and infant formula.

If you plan on feeding both, there are a few points to keep in mind:

1. If both breast and bottle will be offered at one feeding, the baby should be breast-fed first. A supplemental bottle of formula should be offered only after the breasts have been emptied and the baby appears to still be hungry. This pattern provides frequent stimulation to the breasts to maintain milk production and ensures that the baby takes in the fatty calorie-rich breast milk, which is the last to leave the breast. If the bottle is offered first, the satisfied baby is unlikely to feed vigorously and empty the breast.

2. If a breastfeeding mother's schedule makes her unavailable to her baby at the same time everyday, it is possible for her body to adapt to an intermittent feeding schedule. For example, working mothers may want to breast-feed only in the morning before work, in the afternoon after return from work, and throughout the evening and night hours. The alternate caretaker can feed either expressed, stored breast milk or infant formula. After a week or so, the breast-feeding mother may find that her breasts remain "quiet" when she is away from the baby and fill with milk when they are anticipating a feeding. Alternatively, many working mothers express their breast milk with a breast pump while at work, thereby maintaining continuous milk production and a good supply of stored milk for use in their absence. Whether breasts are emptied only intermittently or around the clock, breast milk

leakage is common, and it is wise to wear absorbent nursing pads within the bra.

3. Offering a combination of breast-feedings and bottle feedings with no set pattern is fine too. Occasionally, however, a breast-fed baby will not accept a bottle offered by its mother, insisting instead on the breast. An alternate caretaker may have more success introducing the bottle in that situation. Also, breast-feeding mothers may find their breasts filling up with milk while they are bottle-feeding their baby, leaving them with uncomfortable engorgement. The milk can then be expressed and stored, or the situation can be avoided by having an alternate caretaker offer the bottle feedings.

Breast-feeding

Timing

Your baby should be put to your breast as soon after birth as possible. However, complications during delivery or the postpartum period that delay the baby's suckling should not discourage you.

Your breasts will not begin producing true milk until at least one to two days after delivery. Each time your baby suckles, the sensation will stimulate your brain to make prolactin and oxytocin, the hormones responsible for milk production, "letdown" of milk through the ducts toward the nipples, and uterine contractions. As your milk flows down through the ducts of your breasts, you should feel the letdown sensation as your breasts become engorged with milk. You may also feel tightening in your uterus as it contracts and shrinks back slowly to normal size (a great benefit of breast-feeding!). If your breast milk is slow to come in, it is fine to offer infant formula to feed your hungry baby and maintain her hydration. Putting her to breast during quiet awake periods when she is calm and comfortable will still activate her sucking reflex, which will stimulate your nipples and lead to milk production.

If you do not feel the letdown sensation after several days and your breasts are not engorging or leaking milk, your baby may not be getting enough to drink. You should contact your pediatrician to discuss the need to supplement with formula temporarily until your breast milk is available in good supply.

Breast milk is very easily digestible. It moves through your baby's gastrointestinal tract quite rapidly, which results in the baby feeling hungry again after only a short interval. Though many babies will feed comfortably at three-hour intervals (the time from the *beginning* of one feeding to the *beginning* of the next feeding), it is not unusual for newborns to breast-feed at one-and-one-half- to two-hour intervals. If your baby takes a half hour to feed, he may want to be fed only an hour after the feeding ends. Feeding a newborn on demand is recommended, and it doesn't take long for a baby to settle into a regular and predictable feeding schedule. Newborns should not wait more than four hours between feedings since they cannot regulate their blood sugar level well. Therefore, a baby should be woken for a feeding if four hours have passed since the last feeding.

Babies are extremely variable in their feeding efficiency. An enthusiastic and vigorous feeder may empty its mother's breasts within five minutes, whereas a baby who dozes off frequently or sucks only intermittently may take twenty minutes or more to complete a feeding. If your engorged breasts feel empty at the end of the feeding and your baby is satisfied, it is likely that your baby drank adequate milk, no matter how long the feeding lasted. Good weight gain will confirm adequate intake. The only way to quantify your baby's intake, however, is to express your milk and feed it from a bottle. A general guide to the volume of milk required by a baby is:

(Baby's weight in pounds) divided by two = how many ounces a baby should drink within a four-hour period.

For example, a baby who weighs eight pounds should drink at least four ounces within a four-hour period. If that baby drinks every two hours, he should drink at least two ounces every two hours.

Another simple calculation to determine your baby's milk volume requirement is:

Two to three ounces per pound of body weight = how many ounces a baby should drink in a twenty-four hour period.

Composition and quality

The first fluid that flows from your breasts soon after birth is called "colostrum." It appears as thin, light yellow fluid. It is full of proteins that provide the baby with immunity on the surface of her upper respiratory and gastrointestinal tracts. Once your milk flow is established, the colostrum will no longer be noticeable. It is important never to microwave breast milk, since the valuable infection-fighting proteins in colostrum and mature milk are destroyed by microwave heating. The hind milk (calorie-rich fatty milk) is the last milk to leave the breast before it empties. It is important to allow the baby to empty one breast before offering the other breast, so that he takes in the hind milk. The calories will help him grow, and the fats are important for his developing nervous system. He will also feel more satisfied at the end of the feeding, as if he had a dessert rich in calories and fat!

The quality and quantity of a woman's breast milk is dependent on her own nutrition and hydration status. Many mothers naturally feel hungry and thirsty during breast-feeding, as their bodies notice the fluid and calories they lose in the breast milk. A breast-feeding mother should maintain a well-balanced diet, choosing foods from each food group. Approximately five hundred *extra* calories per day should be consumed to provide adequate nutrition for both mother and baby. Drinking plenty of fluids also helps a mother's body produce an adequate volume of milk for the hungry baby. Breast-feeding mothers should continue a daily multivitamin and mineral supplement.

Both cow milk and human breast milk naturally lack sufficient vitamin D. Cow milk is routinely fortified with vitamin D during processing and therefore becomes a rich source of vitamin D for humans. Since there is no way to fortify human milk in the breast, it is recommended that breast-fed babies begin a liquid supplement that includes vitamin D (e.g., Tri-Vi-Sol) within the first two months. If a breast-fed baby drinks at least sixteen ounces of infant formula daily in addition to breast milk, however, the additional vitamin D supplement is not necessary.

Positioning, technique, and storage

There are several points to keep in mind about breast-feeding techniques:

1. RELAX! Tension will inhibit your milk flow and leads to frustration and more tension.

2. Milk flows from ducts throughout your breast tissue through many openings in your nipples. Your baby's tongue needs to "cup" these milk ducts on the underside of your breast to draw the flow of milk through the channels leading into her mouth. Therefore, it is important for your baby to take as

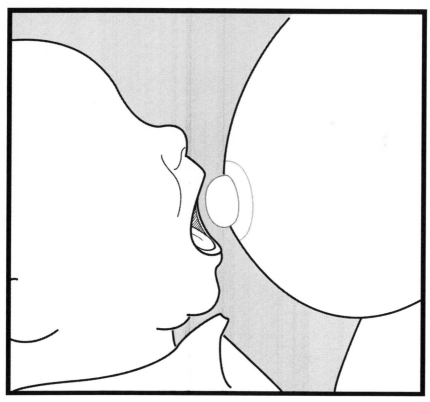

Successful latching on requires a baby to open wide, fitting as much areola and breast in his mouth as possible.

much of your nipple, areola and surrounding breast as possible into her mouth. Be certain that your baby's lower lip is visible on the underside of your breast, and not rolled back into her mouth over her lower gum, limiting extension of the tongue.

3. Proper positioning places your baby's belly against your belly. If your baby's belly faces up and you can see the area of the umbilicus during the feeding, then his neck will need to rotate for his mouth to meet your nipple. Belly-to-belly positioning aligns his mouth directly with your nipple.

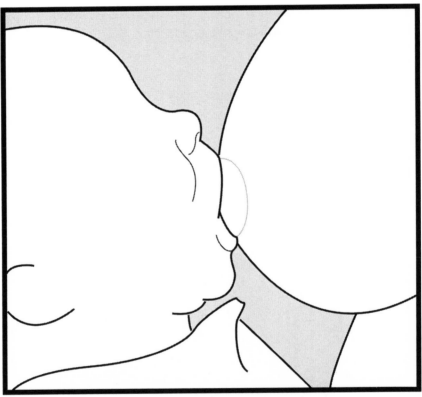

Be sure your baby's lips surround your areola and breast. A lower lip rolled back into the mouth will prevent full extension of the tongue.

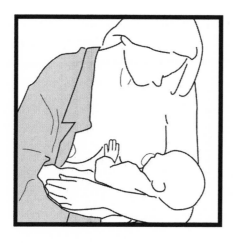

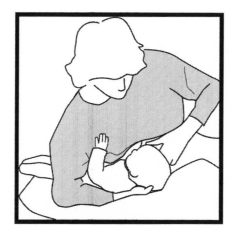

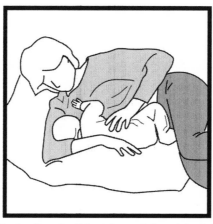

In the cradle hold, the football hold, and the side-lying position, the **89** *baby's mouth should approach the nipple head-on.*

4. The tender skin of your nipples may become very irritated and sore during early breast-feeding. The safest and best products to soothe the skin are lanolin and hind milk (the fat-rich milk at the end of the feeding). As breast-feeding continues, your skin will become much more tolerant to the demands of breast-feeding. Soap should never be used on breast-feeding nipples. They should be rinsed with water only.

5. The breast from which your baby begins each feeding should be completely emptied before the other breast is offered. Then, alternate the breast used to start each feeding. It may be difficult to remember which breast you offered first at the previous feeding. Attaching a safety pin or paperclip to your bra on the side offered first will act as a reminder.

6. If you experience problems with breast-feeding, a "lactation consultant" may be very helpful. Your pediatrician or the hospital where you delivered your baby should be able to refer you to one in your area. The La Leche League offers information and support for breast-feeding mothers on their Web site and may be able to refer a mother to local resources in her area.

Breast milk may also be expressed and fed to your baby through a bottle and artificial nipple. Manual and electric breast pumps are available at a wide range of quality and prices. Many hospitals rent out breast pumps, or they may be purchased at a pharmacy or medical equipment store. Some supermarkets sell low-end breast pumps.

Expressed breast milk is ready to feed. If not used within several hours, it should be stored in the refrigerator and used within one week. For longer storage, it may be kept in a self-contained refrigerator-style freezer compartment for three to four months, or in a deep freezer set below 0°F for six months or more. Breast milk can be stored in special bags designed for that purpose and should be labeled with the storage date. Alternatively, breast milk can be stored in a standard ice-cube tray, which usually creates one-ounce portions. The frozen one-ounce cubes can be removed individually and thawed. Thawed breast milk should not be refrozen, and can be stored in the refrigerator for only one day. Breast milk should never be warmed in a microwave oven, which destroys the valuable immunity proteins found in breast milk and heats unevenly, causing hot spots that can burn a baby's mouth. Frozen or refrigerated milk can be placed in a bowl of warm water or under running warm tap water until it reaches a comfortable temperature. After warming a bottle, shake it gently to distribute the heat and resuspend the cream portion, which separates from the milk and floats to the top. Splash a few drops onto the thin skin of your inner wrist to be sure it has not overheated. It is not necessary to warm milk, though, as most hungry babies will take their milk at room temperature; some will even drink it right out of the refrigerator.

Breast milk jaundice

Occasionally, a breast-feeding infant will develop jaundice at five to seven days of age. Substances in breast milk can interfere with bilirubin clearance from the baby's blood, causing her skin to take on a yellow hue. Discontinuation of breastfeeding is not recommended; rather, the frequency and duration of breastfeeding should be increased. As more milk flows through the baby's intestinal tract, more bilirubin is processed by the liver and passed out of the body with each bowel movement. If your breastfeeding baby develops jaundice, your pediatrician may want to check her blood level of bilirubin. If the level is high, your pediatrician may recommend treatment with phototherapy, which effectively lowers bilirubin levels through the application of visible fluorescent light to the skin.

Formula feeding

Infant formula is a healthy alternative to breast milk for a baby's first year. The Food and Drug Administration regulates infant formulas and all brands must meet certain minimum standards. They are all complete in their protein, carbohydrate, fat, vitamin, and mineral content and are categorized into three groups, based on the source of their protein:

Cow milk formulas contain the proteins whey and casein. Although human breast milk also contains whey and casein, their cow origin makes them distinctly different from human proteins. They are generally well tolerated, though some infants will develop an allergy to the foreign protein. The carbohydrate (or sugar) in cow milk formulas is lactose, which is the same sugar found in human breast milk. Though cow milk formulas do contain cholesterol, most of the fat in infant formula is plant oil (e.g., sunflower, safflower, canola, soy, corn, coconut). Cow milk formulas are recommended as the first choice alternative to human breast milk.

Soy formulas contain soy protein, derived from soybeans. Soy protein is nutritionally incomplete, and all soy formulas include additional necessary proteins. Soy proteins are generally well tolerated, but like cow proteins, may be recognized as foreign by the infant's body. If an infant is already known to be allergic to cow proteins, there is a fifteen percent chance that he will also be allergic to soy protein. Soy formulas are lactose free and their carbohydrates are supplied in the form of corn syrup solids, tapioca starch, or simple sugars. They are cholesterol free and use only plant oils. Soy formulas offer no benefit over cow milk formulas, and are generally only recommended for babies in strict vegetarian families, or for babies who cannot tolerate cow protein or lactose. Premature babies fed soy formulas have weaker bones than those fed human milk or cow milk formula. Therefore, soy protein formulas are not recommended for premature babies.

Hypoallergenic formulas contain proteins in the form of small chains of amino acids, the building blocks of proteins. When proteins are broken down (hydrolyzed) into short amino acid chains, the body cannot recognize them as foreign. They are essentially "predigested" and are very gentle on the gastrointestinal tract. Hypoallergenic formulas are lactose free and contain corn syrup solids, tapioca starch, sucrose, and other simple sugars. They include plant oils and are cholesterol-free. Hypoallergenic formulas are recommended for infants who cannot tolerate cow milk or soy formulas.

Infant formulas are generally available in three forms: ready to feed, liquid concentrate, and powder.

<u>Ready to feed</u> formula requires the least preparation. Simply attach a nipple to the jar, or pour the formula into a bottle of your choice, and it is ready to feed to your baby. It tends to be the most expensive of the three forms. Once opened, it must be kept refrigerated and used within forty-eight hours.

<u>Liquid concentrate</u> requires dilution with water (equal parts concentrated formula and water) prior to feeding. It mixes easily, is less expensive than ready-to-feed formula, and must also be kept refrigerated after opening and used within forty-eight hours. If your house pipes and water supply are clean, there is no reason to boil the water prior to mixing it with your formula. If you have any doubt, consider running the water through a filtering system, using bottled water, or boiling a large volume of tap water for two minutes, which can be stored in the refrigerator for use as needed.

<u>Powdered formula</u> must also be mixed with water. It is sold in either a can or in packets. A can of powder generally includes a scoop, with instructions to add one scoop of powder to each two ounces of water. A packet's instructions will indicate the proper amount of water to add. If bottle markings are to be used to measure the water, it is very important to measure the total water volume first, before adding powder scoops. If powder is added first, the fill line will be reached with less than the right amount of water. Powder formulas are the least expensive and the most portable. They have the longest shelf life and small or large volumes can be mixed as needed. The vigorous shaking required to mix powdered formula creates gas bubbles, and freshly mixed powdered formula should sit briefly to

allow the gas to settle prior to feeding. Once mixed with water, the formula must be used within one hour or refrigerated and used within twenty-four hours.

Infant formulas are not as easily digested as human breast milk, and move through the gastrointestinal tract much more slowly. The interval between feedings, therefore, is longer for formula-fed infants compared to breast-fed babies. Generally, formula-fed babies feed every three to four hours, though some may feed more frequently. The same general rule applies for the minimum volume of formula feedings:

(Baby's weight in pounds) divided by two = how many ounces the baby should drink within a four-hour period

For example, a baby who weighs eight pounds should drink at least four ounces within a four-hour period. If that baby drinks every two hours, he should drink at least two ounces every two hours.

In a twenty-four hour period, a baby should consume two to three ounces of infant formula per pound of body weight.

Bottles and nipples

Bottle and nipple technology has boomed! You will find many options in bottle shapes and sizes, bag inserts, and anti-gas mechanisms. The most important rule about bottle-feeding involves positioning of the baby and the bottle. The baby should never be bottle-fed in a supine (lying down flat on his back) position with the bottle propped. It is very difficult for a baby to control the constant flow of milk dripping into his mouth, and his airway may be in danger if he cannot free himself from the bottle. The best feeding position for the baby is a comfortable 45°. The bottle should be angled to ensure that formula, not air, fills the tip of the nipple. A baby who swallows air instead of formula through the nipple will have a lot of gas to pass!

Nipples are available in a variety of shapes, hole sizes, configurations and flow speeds. Generally, the success of bottle feeding is more dependent on the nipple than the bottle. Most nipple packages will indicate an age range for which they are intended. For successful feeding, your baby's lips should rest on the widest portion of the nipple, and the milk should be deposited deep toward the back of the tongue and throat. A nipple that is too large or too small will lead to either gagging or frustration. Nipple packages also indicate hole configuration and flow speed. The best bottle and nipple combination for your baby can be determined only by trying them out. If your baby feeds well with the first one you try, there is no need to purchase one of each kind. Just stick with what works! If you plan to feed from both your breast and a bottle, some experts recommend establishing exclusive breast-feeding for two to four weeks before introducing the bottle. Pulling milk out from a breast requires a sucking mechanism that is entirely different (and more difficult) than sucking milk from an artificial nipple. A baby without a well-developed preference for the breast may not put forth the effort required to breast-feed, knowing that milk flows much more easily from a bottle. Generally, though, a few bottles of infant formula early on will not ruin the chances of successful breast-feeding.

There is no need to sterilize the bottles and nipples by boiling. Regular cleaning with hot soapy water or in a hot dishwasher cycle is adequate. Bottles and nipples should be washed prior to first use.

If your baby has difficulty feeding with any nipple you offer, she may have a structural, functional, or muscular problem in her mouth or jaw. Your pediatrician should be consulted.

* * *

Temperature Control

Before birth, babies are kept warm in the womb by their mother's body temperature, approximately 98.6°F. At birth, they are thrust out into air that is nearly 30°F cooler and must rely on their own bodies to generate heat. In the delivery room, they are dried off and swaddled. In the hospital nursery, they may be placed naked under a radiant warmer if they have difficulty maintaining an adequate body temperature. Babies that are premature tend to have more difficulty, but even full-term babies may need help staying warm early on. A baby who is cold will have a body temperature less than 97°F and may have purple-colored hands and feet.

The best ways to keep a baby warm are:

1. Keep the room temperature comfortable, around 68–70°F.

2. Dress your baby in layers—consider using a "onesie" (a one-piece T-shirt that fastens between the legs) or T-shirt beneath another outfit, and a swaddling or receiving blanket on top.

3. Cover the head with a snug-fitting cap (quite a bit of body heat is lost from the head, especially if it is bald!).

4. Cover the feet in booties or socks.

Just as a baby may have difficulty maintaining warmth, a baby who is overbundled may have difficulty cooling down. Generally, babies are comfortable with one light layer added to the same amount of clothing that keeps most other people comfortable. If your baby feels hot or has a body temperature over 100.4°F measured with a thermometer in the rectum, consider whether or not you have overdressed him. If, by removing layers, his temperature quickly normalizes, then he should be re-dressed with fewer layers. If his high temperature persists, or if he has any additional signs or symptoms of illness, you must consult your pediatrician.

Rectal temperatures are considered the most accurate measurement of a baby's body temperature. Glass mercury thermometers are no longer recommended, but plastic digital thermometers are safe, accurate, and inexpensive. To measure your baby's temperature rectally:

1. Place your baby on her belly and unfasten her diaper so that her buttocks are exposed.

2. Remove any cap or cover from your digital thermometer and place a small amount of petroleum jelly or A+D ointment on the tip for lubrication.

3. With one hand, spread your baby's buttocks apart to expose her anus.

4. Activate the thermometer—there is usually a button to press—and gently insert the thermometer into the anus just beyond the point where the silver tip is no longer visible, not farther than ¾ of an inch. *Never force the thermometer through resistance.*

5. Press your baby's buttocks closed against each other with one hand while keeping the thermometer in place with the other hand.

6. When the thermometer beeps, remove it from your baby's anus and read the temperature displayed in the window.

If you are uncomfortable measuring your baby's temperature in the rectum, place the thermometer tip deep into the armpit (axilla). Use the same method as above (no lubricant needed), holding the arm close against the chest until the thermometer beeps. Generally, one degree should be added to an axillary temperature to reflect the true body temperature.

* * *

Comfort and Soothing

All babies need comfort and soothing. "Comfort" is provided through warmth, cleaning, feeding, and adequate sleep; "soothing" is any intervention that restores calm to a baby who is expressing distress. Sucking is a reflex that babies are born with, which, in addition to promoting successful feeding, is their primary means of soothing. Babies have a need for a certain amount of "nonnutritive" sucking, and caretakers must not interpret every sucking motion to be a demand for food. Some babies will find their thumb, fingers, or hand very early and learn to soothe themselves. For those who don't, a pacifier is an effective alternative. Available in many different shapes and sizes, pacifiers have two important parts: the handle or face portion and the sucker. Face portions should not be too irritating to the skin around the mouth and should not obstruct the flow of air through the baby's nose. However, they must be large enough not to slip into the mouth and pose a choking hazard. Suckers may be straight nipple shaped, bulbous, or "orthodontic," which includes a dip in the area that passes under the top gum and an upturned tip that fits into the roof of the baby's mouth. Any sucker style is fine, as long as its role is limited to pacification. A pacifier used beyond times of need becomes a constant mouth plug and a bad habit. Generally, pacifiers are no longer necessary after six months of age. At that time, babies have lost their sucking reflex and are able to reach and locate objects that provide a soothing effect within their environment. It is also the time when teeth begin erupting. Therefore, if you offer your baby a pacifier as a newborn, you should plan to discontinue its use by six months of age. Remember, pacifiers should not be attached to a baby with a long string or cord, which is a strangulation hazard.

Within the first few weeks, most newborns like to be swaddled in a blanket. Any blanket can be used to swaddle a newborn, but the thin receiving blankets allow the tightest wrap, replicating the familiar feeling of being in the womb. To swaddle a baby:

1. Lay the blanket on a flat surface with one corner turned down, pointing toward the center of the blanket.

2. Place the baby on the blanket slightly off center to one side, aligning the straight edge of the turned-down corner with the bottom of his ears.

3. Pull the short side corner of the blanket across his body and tuck it in behind his hips.

4. Fold the bottom of the blanket up his body so that the bottom edge lies across his chest or abdomen.

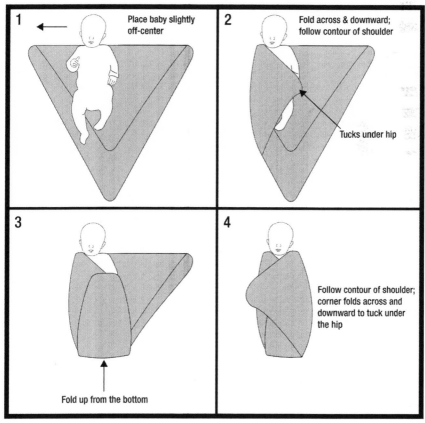

Many newborns like to be swaddled.

5. Pull the remaining side corner across the baby's body and tuck it behind him to complete the wrap.

If your baby seems uncomfortable, make sure your wrap is not too tight. Keep in mind that some babies do not like to be swaddled, and prefer to be held in loose blankets or no blankets at all.

* * *

Stimulation

Stimulation, in the world of a newborn, is any experience involving the baby's senses. Only a few sensations, such as the in-utero sound of a heartbeat, voices, music, or feeling rhythmic movements, are familiar to a newborn at birth. All other experiences will be new to the baby and qualify as stimulation. Examples include hearing birds sing or rain fall, feeling a warm breeze or a gentle massage, and watching a face full of expressions or a brightly colored mobile. Stimulation is necessary for the development of a baby's brain, vision, motor skills, emotion, and social interactions. Stimulation will also help to establish healthy sleeping patterns.

Your newborn will spend most of her time eating and sleeping for the first few weeks. Even so, your baby's senses are well developed and any sensory input helps to stimulate growth of the brain. Early on, sensory stimulation is most often provided in the form of talking/ singing, patting, swinging, or rocking. "Tummy time," or placing your baby on her tummy while she is awake, is the best motor exercise for a baby. This prone position works the neck, shoulders, and abdominal muscles, and a brightly colored, multi-textured activity mat placed beneath the baby can provide more sensory stimulation. Since your baby's vision is not well developed, visual stimulation is limited to nearby, brightly colored or contrasted objects or the recognizable form of a human face. Over several weeks, your baby will spend much more time awake and alert and will be very receptive to new sensory experiences. Infant massage is a great way to provide multi-sensory stimulation through eye contact, singing or talking, and using scented plant oils while gently rubbing the skin and muscles of the baby's entire body. Caretakers must always keep in mind that any new experience, no matter how mundane, qualifies as stimulation. Prolonged or extreme stimulation can be irritating to a baby, and plenty of time should be allowed for sleeping and quiet relaxation.

* * *

Checkups

If you delivered your baby in a hospital, it is likely he was examined several times during his nursery stay by a health professional. Babies should not be released from a hospital nursery until they are at least twenty-four hours old; it is preferable to keep a baby in the hospital for at least forty-eight to seventy-two hours. Generally, a baby's discharge coincides with the mother's discharge, which often is determined by the mode of delivery (forty-eight to seventy-two hours following vaginal delivery and seventy-two to ninety-six hours after Cesarean section). It is commonly recommended for the baby to see a pediatric health professional within two to three days after hospital nursery discharge. You may be asked to schedule a follow-up appointment only one day after hospital discharge in the following situations:

1. Your baby is being discharged from the hospital after only twenty-four hours.

2. Your baby had some difficulty in the newborn nursery such as frequent spitting up, slow feeding, breast-feeding difficulty, or some other problem that may require further evaluation if persistent.

3. Your baby has jaundice and requires a repeat bilirubin measurement and a physical assessment of his condition.

Newborn exams focus on:

1. Weight: Babies lose approximately five to ten percent of their weight in the first few days after birth. They are then expected to regain the lost weight by seven to ten days of age. Your pediatrician will be very interested in your baby's weight and the pattern of feeding.

2. Urine and stool output: Your pediatrician will be interested in your baby's urine and stool output, stool color, and consistency.

3. Head: assessing the skull, including the fontanels (soft spots), sutures (separations between the moveable bones of the skull), and size of the skull; checking the eyes for normal shape, placement, pupil size and function, and the "red reflex," which reflects the health of the retina or back surface of the eyes; checking his lips and palate (roof of the mouth) for clefts or defects; and checking for proper placement and formation of the ears.

4. Neck: Checking for any small opening in the neck or any tight muscles.

5. Chest: Listening to the heart for any abnormal rhythm or additional sounds (murmurs); listening to the lungs for normal air movement. Feeling the clavicles (bones that connect the breastbone to the shoulders) for cracking during delivery.

6. Abdomen: Listening for normal gurgling sounds; feeling for any abnormal organ (e.g., liver, spleen, kidney, bladder) enlargement; and checking the condition of the umbilical cord.

7. Back: Examining the spine for straightness and for abnormally deep dimples, creases, or hair tufts at the base of the spine near the buttocks.

8. Genitals: Examining boys' scrotums to confirm the presence of two testicles; examining the tip of the penis and foreskin for normal placement of the urethral opening (through which urine flows) in the center and checking the circumcision wound if performed; confirming proper length of the penis; in girls, checking the clitoris for proper size; and checking the anus for normal elastic tone and reflex tightening when touched.

9. Hips: Checking for proper placement and stability of the femur (thigh bone) within the hip joint.

10. Arms and Legs: Counting the fingers and toes; looking for any deformities in the structures of the bones or digits; feeling for pulses in all four extremities.

11. Skin: Looking for newborn markings and rashes; assessing the color of the skin.

12. Nervous system: Checking your baby's reflexes, muscle tone, and symmetry of movement.

* * *

Choosing your pediatrician or health care provider

If you chose your pediatrician before you delivered your baby, simply call his or her office and request a newborn follow-up appointment. If you did not choose your pediatrician before you delivered your baby, you must now do so. Your choice of pediatricians depends on several factors:

Insurance: You should choose a pediatrician who accepts your insurance plan. You can usually get a list of participating physicians from your insurance provider manual, your insurance company's Web site, or by speaking to a client service representative over the phone. If you are uninsured, you may request help from the hospital social work department to enroll in low-cost insurance or Medicaid if you qualify.

Location: Your pediatrician should not be too far from where you live. Traveling with your baby can be cumbersome, and when your baby grows into a young child (with or without a new younger sibling), you may dread long car rides to the doctor's office. Many hospitals will have a referral service with a listing of local physicians who are affiliated with the hospital and have offices nearby. On the other hand, you may know an outstanding physician who's worth the trip!

Word of mouth: Many mothers choose a pediatrician because they have heard great things about him or her. A friend, neighbor, family member, your obstetrician, or an acquaintance from a prenatal class may recommend a pediatrician who is near your home and takes your insurance. If you live where you grew up, you may look into bringing your baby to the pediatrician you visited as a child!

Office policies: Physician offices differ in their hours of operation, weekend, nighttime, and holiday availability, wait times for appointment scheduling, availability of certain individual physicians (in a group practice), phone advice policy, wait times for school forms, lateness policy, and separation of sick and healthy children in the waiting area, among other details. If you are choosing your physician based on the operation of his or her office, you should really take time *before* your baby is born to research several local offices until you find one that fits your needs. Most offices can give you the information over the phone, and may invite you in to meet the office staff and pediatricians.

Many states post information about physicians licensed and registered within their state on their Web sites.

Consumers can review a physician's educational background, clinical training, and Board certification status, an accomplishment earned through a process of arduous testing and ongoing education within each specialty. In addition, office locations, foreign language capabilities, accepted insurance plans, malpractice history, and local hospital affiliations may be listed.

At any point, if you are not satisfied with your new pediatrician, say so. Pediatricians and parents share the same goal of keeping a child healthy, safe, and happy, and must be able to communicate openly and honestly. A child does not benefit when the relationship between the physician and the child's family is uncomfortable, strained, or dissatisfying in any way. It is not uncommon for patients to switch doctors for a variety of reasons. Whatever the cause of your dissatisfaction, consider talking to the office manager or your pediatrician. Depending on your situation, they may have a satisfactory solution. If not, they would probably appreciate notification that your child will no longer be a patient in their practice. Occasionally, it is the *physician* who feels uncomfortable with a patient or feels unable to provide what a family requests or requires. That physician may ask the patient to find a new doctor. For whatever reason you find yourself switching pediatricians, remember to request that a copy of your child's medical record be sent to your new pediatrician.

After your first newborn follow-up visit, your pediatrician will tell you when to schedule your baby's next appointment.

8
CAPABILITIES AND LIMITATIONS

Whatever expectations you have for your child, such as athletic skill, superior intellect or great celebrity potential, put them on hold. The only abilities that nature supplies to newborns are those necessary to ensure their survival. As the first month passes by, your baby will slowly develop motor, social, language and adaptive skills required to interact with her physical and social environment. But for now…

What newborn babies can do:

Babies communicate their needs by crying. The loud, irritating sound of a baby crying is nature's way of ensuring that a baby is tended to, and his needs are met. If a cry sounded pleasant, then babies would not be fed, diapers would not be changed, and urgent medical conditions may go unnoticed. Needs that elicit a cry response include hunger, discomfort (wetness, fever, pain), tiredness, and a need for soothing. Many parents can distinguish their baby's different needs based on the pattern or pitch of the cry. When your baby cries, consider her needs: has it been several hours since she was last fed; is her wet diaper irritating her sensitive skin; was she burped well enough after her recent feeding? Remember that soothing (which may be in the form of being held and rocked) is a *need* for newborns. If your baby is crying and you are too tired to meet your baby's needs or feel frustrated or angry in your sleep-deprived state, request the help of a good friend or relative. A short break from parenthood to take an overdue nap will help you deal more easily with your baby's crying. If your baby is crying inconsolably despite all needs being met, there may be a more serious problem and you should contact your pediatrician.

Babies can indicate they're done feeding by turning their heads away from the nipple. When your baby turns his mouth away from the nipple, believe him. If he has not taken his usual amount, his stomach may be full of air. Successful burping may result in a return of his appetite and acceptance of the nipple. Forcing the last drop out of the bottle after your baby signals he's done can result in excessive spitting up and uncomfortable regurgitation or gastroesophageal reflux. Regurgitated milk mixed with stomach acid can threaten the airway and interfere with breathing, which may be a serious situation. Falling asleep during a feeding is different from actively turning away from the nipple. If your baby is constantly falling asleep during feeds, try stimulating him by rubbing his back, tapping the bottoms of his feet, or repositioning him. If his intake remains minimal through several feedings, he is at risk for dehydration and poor weight gain, and should be brought to the attention of a pediatrician.

Babies can turn their heads from side to side when they lie on their bellies. Tummy time is extremely important for babies and, when supervised, is a safe activity. Placing a baby on her belly *while she is awake* is a great way to exercise her neck, shoulders, upper back, and abdominal muscles, which also aids in digestion. A clean, firm, flat surface, such as a carpeted floor covered by a baby blanket or towel, makes a great exercise area. She may get upset and frustrated with her limited abilities, but the exercise will lead to increasing strength and achievement of new skills. If she decides to get comfortable and fall asleep, she should be turned over onto her back, as recommended for SIDS prevention.

Newborn babies smile in their sleep. The purpose of the sleeping smile is unclear; many attribute the occurrences to passage of gas. Nature may have programmed babies to smile spontaneously and unpredictably to capture the attention and affection of caregivers. Many parents find themselves watching their sleeping babies, waiting for a smile at any moment. Seeing your baby's smile now and then makes the long days (and nights) of responding to long, loud cries and feeding, diapering, and holding, a lot more rewarding. The usual age range for babies to develop a meaningful or "social" smile in response to another individual is between two weeks and two months of age.

Babies can make associations. An "association" connects two ideas or feelings in the mind. Associations allow your baby to predict circumstances, which builds confidence and trust in her world. One of the most important associations you will want to foster in your baby is the connection of sleep to a brief ritual or cue. Many families with newborns find themselves holding the baby constantly, allowing the baby to fall asleep while being held, following a feeding and a burping. The routine of *feed-burp-sleep,* six or eight times each day becomes a routine the baby anticipates, and an opportunity to develop an association. Introducing the same additional cue every time the baby is expected to fall asleep can lead to an association of that particular cue with sleep. Cues may be in the form of a particular song or background noise, a short baby book, a scent, a lighting situation or a physical object such as a blanket or soft doll. Without an additional cue, a baby will focus on the association of the feeding, burping and rocking prior to sleep. Several months later, you will find your baby unable to go down to sleep without a feeding, burping, and rocking. Therefore, it is helpful to establish a sleep association cue as early in life as possible.

What newborn babies cannot do:

Newborn babies cannot understand or speak English (or any other language). Although it is very important to talk or sing frequently to your baby, it is unreasonable to expect him to understand anything you say. Babies do not even recognize and respond to their own name until close to eight months of age, do not follow simple one-step commands until close to their first birthday, and cannot make requests. It is your responsibility to become familiar with your baby's needs and provide complete care, expecting very little cooperation in return.

Newborns do not learn good behavior through discipline. Newborn babies are incapable of understanding right and wrong, and no attempt should be made to discipline a baby. Excessive loud crying, holding tight fists (sometimes including someone's dangling hair), spitting up on a fresh outfit, soiling a freshly placed diaper, and other inconvenient or unexpected occurrences are all within the realm of normal newborn activity and do not deserve punishment.

9
TROUBLESHOOTING

Breast-feeding difficulty

The art and science of breast-feeding is a specialty unto itself. Lactation consultants are certified professionals who assist lactating mothers toward the goal of successful breast-feeding. Many hospitals have lactation consultants on-site in their maternity wards or can refer mothers to local lactation consultants. Some insurance companies will include coverage of the service in their benefits. La Leche League is a national organization whose mission is to promote breast-feeding as the best nutrition for babies and provide services and support for breast-feeding mothers who are experiencing difficulty.

Difficulty latching on: Babies may have difficulty latching on for a variety of reasons. A very common problem is improper positioning. Belly-to-belly is the best position as the baby approaches the nipple across the mother's lap. Resting the baby on a firm pillow or cushion placed in the mother's lap may help with proper positioning. When the baby's belly faces the mother's belly, his mouth faces the nipple head-on so that his neck does not twist. If the baby was born by Cesarean section, it may be more comfortable for the mother to hold the baby like a football on the side she is nursing. This position avoids placing the baby over the surgical wound. It is still important for the baby's mouth to approach the nipple straight, without twisting his neck. Proper latching on also requires the baby's mouth to open wide so that a large portion of the nipple and areola (the thin, colored area surrounding the nipple) extends far into the baby's mouth. Always be sure that your baby's lower lip is not rolled back into his mouth over his lower gum, which limits the extension of the tongue. If your baby's mouth does not open wide, stroking his chin or cheeks may make the mouth open wider.

Flat or inverted nipples: Nipples that are flat do not elongate easily into the baby's mouth. The baby therefore cannot cup his mouth around the ducts of the breast and draw milk into his mouth. Breast engorgement flattens nipples much the way a balloon becomes tense and less elastic as it is overfilled. Expressing a small amount of milk just before feeding will allow the breast to soften and the nipple to elongate more easily. "Breast shells" are thin plastic cups with a central hole placed over the nipple, held in place with the bra. When worn inside the bra between feedings, the nipple is trained to take a more elongated shape. Ice applied to your nipples, rolling your nipples between two fingers, or pumping will also cause them to become erect.

Sore or cracked nipples: Proper positioning and latching on will help to minimize the nipple discomfort many mothers experience during early breast-feeding. If your nipples do become sore or cracked, first consider whether or not your baby is positioned properly, tummy-to-tummy. Also, never clean your nipples with soap, which may lead to drying and further irritation.

Lanolin is a cream which is soothing to sore, cracked nipples, which is also safe for the baby during breast-feeding. Lastly, rubbing the rich, fatty hind milk over the nipples at the end of each feeding will soothe sore nipples. Over time, your nipples will become more tolerant to the demands of breast-feeding.

Swollen, painful breasts; mastitis; abscess: Breasts that are fully engorged with milk are uncomfortable. Generally, emptying milk from the breast, either by allowing the baby to nurse or expressing milk with a pump, gives great relief. Mastitis occurs when milk ducts remain engorged and become plugged, not allowing milk to flow easily. Additional symptoms of mastitis include fever, chills, and fatigue. A warm compress and gentle massage may loosen the plugged ducts and allow milk to flow normally. If the ducts remain inflamed, bacteria entering the skin through small cracks may lead to infection and possibly abscess formation. Infections that develop are generally treated with antibiotics; occasionally a pus-filled cavity requires surgical drainage. If your breasts develop painful, hard areas that do not improve after expressing milk, applying warm compresses, and massage, you should consult your obstetrician. If your physician prescribes an antibiotic, be sure to inquire about the safety of continuing to breastfeed while taking the medication.

Poor milk production: The body's production of milk operates on the principle of supply and demand. The more your baby demands milk (demonstrated by frequent nursing and emptying of the breast), the more milk your body will produce to meet that demand. However, other factors also influence milk

115

production. Since milk is mostly fluid, your body may feel very thirsty while breast-feeding, and it is a good idea to drink whenever your baby drinks, to replace the fluid. Stress also influences milk production and it is important to be comfortable and relaxed while breast-feeding. Some medications and drugs, including alcohol, also suppress milk production, and you should check with your doctor or your baby's pediatrician before taking medicines if you are breast-feeding.

Preference for one breast: Occasionally, a baby will seem to have a strong preference to nurse from only one particular breast. Offering the less-favored side when the baby is most hungry may work to re-establish a liking for both sides. Alternatively, the problem may not be in your breasts, but in your baby's preference to lie on one side more than the other. Consider repositioning the baby so that he remains lying on his preferred side (accomplished by a "football hold"). If repositioning does not work, consider expressing your milk from the side not favored and offering it from a bottle.

* * *

Breathing difficulty

Breathing difficulty in a newborn is a complaint taken very seriously by pediatricians. The breathing process is influenced by the nose and mouth, upper and lower airways, lungs, heart, brain, muscles, and abdomen. Conditions such as fever, anemia, infection, and dehydration also influence a baby's breathing pattern. Any concern that your baby is not breathing easily, especially if she is having difficulty feeding, warrants a call to your pediatrician.

Nasal congestion: Nasal congestion is a very common occurrence among newborns. There are several reasons why a baby may develop nasal congestion. First, babies develop in a liquid in-utero environment, where fluid fills their noses and respiratory tracts. At birth, their noses are suctioned, and over the first few weeks they sneeze frequently to force out any remaining fluid. Also, babies very frequently "reflux" their feedings (wet burping or occasionally vomiting). Since the nose is continuous with the mouth and throat, refluxed milk very often gets deposited in the nose. Milk fats and proteins accumulate and mix with mucous produced by the irritated membranes, forming thick plugs. Another cause of nasal congestion is a common cold or viral infection, transmitted from another person. Whatever the cause of the nasal congestion, the treatment in each case involves normal saline nose drops and suctioning with a bulb syringe.

"Normal saline" is a saltwater solution in a concentration that is most compatible with our bodies. It is unmedicated and can be used liberally without concern of overdosing. It is available without a prescription in most supermarkets and drug stores, and goes by many different brand names, as well as store brand or generic. It is available in drops and spray; drops are more practical for use in young babies. A bulb syringe is a rubber suction device in the shape of a light bulb. Some mothers are hesitant to use saline drops with a bulb syringe because the babies cry and do not enjoy it. It is very helpful, though, and, despite the brief period of discomfort, it is generally very effective at relieving nasal congestion. The procedure should be performed quickly as follows:

1. Place the baby on his back on a flat surface, such as a crib or changing table, with your saline bottle and bulb syringe nearby. Moveable surfaces such as swings, rocking cradles, and bouncy seats are too unstable and you will find yourself chasing a moving target.

2. Prepare: remove the cap from the saline drops. Have your bulb syringe nearby and have a cloth or tissue available to discard the suctioned mucous.

3. Holding the baby's head still, squeeze one to two drops of normal saline into each nostril.

4. Put the bottle of saline down and pick up the bulb syringe so that the bulbous portion fills the palm of your hand.

5. Squeeze the air out of the bulb syringe. Maintaining your squeeze, gently place the pointed portion of the bulb syringe into one of the baby's nostrils while gently pressing the other nostril closed. Insert the tip of the bulb syringe as far back as possible, but stop if and when you meet resistance. With the tip of the bulb syringe still in the baby's nostril, allow the bulb portion to expand by opening your squeeze. As the bulb expands, nasal secretions will be sucked into the bulb.

6. Remove the bulb syringe and squeeze the suctioned secretions onto a cloth or tissue.
Repeat the procedure on the other nostril. If more secretions remain in the nose, repeat suctioning. It is important to be gentle, though, as nasal membranes are delicate. If a small amount of blood is noticed in the secretion, discontinue suctioning at that time to allow the membranes to heal.

Rapid breathing: The normal respiratory rate for newborn babies is thirty to fifty breaths per minute. Babies will occasionally have brief periods of very rapid, shallow breathing during sleep, which is a normal occurrence. During that time, they should be comfortable with good color and no distress. However, if your baby is breathing rapidly while awake or has poor color (dusky or pale), is in distress, has difficulty feeding, inconsolable irritability, fever or cough, your baby should be brought to medical attention. Abnormally rapid breathing may indicate a problem in the lungs or heart, or may indicate conditions such as infection, anemia, or a disturbance in the acid and base balance of the body.

Gasping or not breathing: Watching a baby gasp or stop breathing is frightening. Newborns normally have episodes of "periodic breathing" during sleep. Respiratory pauses last for five to ten seconds, then breathing resumes at a rapid, then normal, rate. Babies sleep comfortably through the episodes, and periodic breathing has no detrimental effect on a baby. Occasionally, though, a baby's gasp is accompanied by choking or vomiting, stiffening, eyes widening or rolling, color change to red, dusky, or pale, or limpness.

Commonly, a caretaker's response is to stimulate the baby by shaking him gently, blowing in his face, or quickly repositioning him and patting his back. Occasionally, caretakers call 9-1-1 for emergency assistance and it is not uncommon for babies to be brought to a local hospital emergency department for evaluation.

Even if your baby's gasping episode was brief and he now appears well, the episode should be brought to the attention of your pediatrician. Many conditions can cause a baby to gasp for breath. These include:

1. Most commonly, <u>gastroesophageal reflux disease (GERD)</u>: stomach contents flow back up the esophagus (tube connecting the throat to the stomach). The area in the throat where the esophagus begins is very close to the area where the breathing tube begins with the larynx (voice box). In the process of GERD, the stomach contents ascend toward the vicinity of the larynx. The baby's body responds to the threat of stomach contents approaching the airway by spasming and closing the larynx. Air cannot pass through a closed larynx, and the baby is unable to breathe. If the larynx does not spasm, the refluxing stomach contents may enter the airway, another mechanism by which GERD interferes with breathing. GERD management includes feeding small volumes at frequent intervals, effective burping, upright positioning following each feed, avoiding constipation (which prevents the forward flow of intestinal contents), thickening the milk (generally with rice cereal), and antacid medication, if necessary. If your baby has GERD, your

pediatrician should determine the most appropriate course of treatment.

2. A seizure, or abnormal electrical activity in the brain, is a much less common cause of gasping or breathing difficulty in babies. Newborn babies who seize often stiffen, shake, roll their eyes, drool, vomit, and change their color to red or dusky. They may remain lethargic for a short time following the episode.

3. Infections can cause a baby to stop breathing or gasp. Urinary tract infections are the most common infections to cause this symptom in a baby who otherwise appears well. Respiratory infections, blood infections, or meningitis (infection of the fluid surrounding the brain and spinal cord) can also cause gasping or episodes of not breathing, but babies with these infections often look much sicker.

4. Heart problems rarely cause a baby to gasp or stop breathing.

* * *

Colic

Colic is defined by episodes of unexplained crying, which last for three or more hours on three or more days of the week. Colic often worsens in the late afternoon or early evening hours, after the baby has been comfortable and feeding well all day. It generally develops toward the end of the first month, peaks in intensity at six weeks of age, and disappears by three months. The cause of colic is not known. It is *not* caused by gas, although a gassy baby may also have periods of crying. Some experts believe it is a stage in the development of the baby's nervous system. Not all babies get colic, and those who do may have many colic-free days also. Calming a colicky baby can be difficult. Some techniques to try include:

1. Place your baby in a continuous motion swing or vibrating seat.

2. Take your baby on a car ride.

3. Place your baby on top of a vibrating washing machine (*your baby must be secured safely in an infant seat with no danger of falling and you must stay nearby your baby!).

4. Stand up, holding your baby close, and move your baby around rhythmically by gently twisting your body or bending your knees up and down.

All of these techniques require motion, and you may have to try many different techniques before you figure out what works best. If no simple technique works, your baby may have a problem other than colic. Other common reasons for newborn crying include gas pains, constipation, gastroesophageal reflux disease, skin rashes or sores (make sure baby's skin did not get caught in a zipper!), hair tourniquets (a strand of hair wrapped tightly around a finger or toe), too-tight elastic, foreign objects in the eye (such as an eyelash), or the beginning of an infection. You should undress your baby completely and examine her for any cause of discomfort. If there is no obvious problem, and your baby remains inconsolable, you should contact your pediatrician.

* * *

Color changes

Throughout the first month, a baby's skin goes through many changes. Some very common color changes include:

Dark red or purple extremities: A baby's extremities (hands and feet) will appear darker red or purplish if they are cool. Warming them up with socks, mittens, or bundling should return their color to match the rest of their body.

Red face: A baby crying vigorously may seem to hold the cry in an exhalation phase and may turn red or dark in the face. The forceful exhalation temporarily suspends blood flow back to the heart, and the dark venous blood accumulates. Once the baby begins a new breath, his color should improve. Bearing down for a bowel movement results in the same effect, but is usually seen in an older age group, whose abdominal muscles are more developed.

Yellow skin: Jaundice is a condition in which the breakdown product of red blood cells (bilirubin) accumulates, causing the skin and the whites of the eyes to turn yellow. Babies are born with extra blood, which normally breaks down after birth, causing mild jaundice at two to three days of age (termed physiologic jaundice). Jaundice clears when the bilirubin is processed in the liver and removed from the body through the stool. Bilirubin is what gives color to stool, and it is normal for babies to have rich golden or mustard-colored stool as they clear the bilirubin from their bodies. Occasionally, when a baby's blood breakdown is excessive, the bilirubin level goes very high, and the yellow skin color intensifies. Factors that contribute to excessive jaundice include prematurity, Asian race, bleeding or bruising, blood type mismatching between the mother and the baby, and breast-feeding. If any of these factors is present or if your baby appears to be very jaundiced, your pediatrician may want to check your baby's bilirubin level through a simple blood test. Frequent feeding, which promotes passage of stool, is the best way to clear the yellow color from your baby's skin. If the level is very high, though, your pediatrician may recommend phototherapy, which applies visible fluorescent light to the baby's skin to help clear the bilirubin and resolve the jaundice. *If your baby's skin is yellow and he is passing stool that is pale or clay colored, your baby may have a problem processing bilirubin in the liver. Your pediatrician should be consulted promptly.*

Marbling (physiologic cutis marmorata) appears as red, purple, and normal flesh tone in a net-like pattern. It is very often transient and is a normal variation when the baby is cold, but otherwise well. Warming your baby should help to resolve the marbled pattern of the skin. If your baby is not acting well (feeding poorly, crying excessively, vomiting, or lethargic) or has a fever, consult your pediatrician.

Harlequin coloring: Occasionally, one half of a baby's body may appear pale while the other half has normal or dark red coloration, with the two halves sharply demarcated. This harlequin coloration is a benign process that lasts seconds or minutes and has no meaning or impact on the baby's health.

* * *

Constipation

A newborn's pattern of bowel movements is variable. Generally, breast-fed babies pass stool more frequently (sometimes after each feeding) than formula-fed babies, who may pass stool only once per day or every other day. Whatever the pattern, newborn stool should be very soft with a texture anywhere between mustard and cookie batter. Stool that is very hard, or accumulates to a large mass before passing, may tear the inner lining of the rectum or anus. Streaks of blood may then be noticeable on the outside of the stool. If you believe your baby is constipated based on either the pattern or consistency of the stool, it helps to consider the processes involved in normal stool output:

Digestion of food: As milk moves through the intestinal tract, nutrients and water are absorbed into the body through the small intestine and additional water is absorbed into the body through the large intestine, before stool is passed through the anus. Breast milk is more easily digested than formula, and spends much less time in the intestinal tract before it is evacuated. Therefore, it retains more of its water content and passes as softer and thinner stool than that of a formula-fed baby. If your formula-fed baby is passing infrequent, hard stools, a *small* amount of water (not more than one ounce twice daily) may help. Adding one-half teaspoon of brown sugar to the water may help even more (remember that honey and corn syrup are not safe alternatives, and should not be fed to infants). Digestibility of milk may also be affected by the source of the protein. If your formula-fed baby has difficulty digesting proteins that come from a cow or soy source, your pediatrician may recommend a formula made with proteins that are already broken down. Cow or soy proteins may affect a breast-fed baby if the mother's diet includes cow protein (including beef), dairy, or soy products, which pass into breast milk. Eliminating cow protein, soy, or both from the mother's diet may make the breast milk much more easily digestible.

Muscle movement within the walls of the intestines: Intestines are lined by muscles, which contract in waves to move food in the forward direction (peristalsis). Intestinal muscles are much more active when the body is awake, and tend to rest when the body is asleep. They are stimulated by food entering the stomach (a gastro-colic reflex), which explains why many babies will pass a bowel movement after each feeding. Touching the outside of the anus with a lubricated thermometer or Q-tip also stimulates the intestinal muscles through sensory nerves. Intestinal muscle activity is controlled mostly by its rich nerve supply and the metabolic rate of the body, including the thyroid gland. Certain drugs or medications can also affect the muscular activity of the intestines. If your baby has always had very infrequent bowel movements and uncomfortable abdominal distension, you should discuss the possibility of an intestinal muscle, innervation, or metabolism issue with your pediatrician.

Pushing ability of the abdominal wall muscles: As you can recall from your own experience, passing a bowel movement requires some pushing from your abdominal muscles, which is easiest from a squatting position. Although babies are born with good tone (related to a healthy nervous system), they have very little strength in their muscles. The best way to exercise a baby's abdominal muscles is to place her on a firm surface on her belly (only while she is awake). As she lifts her arms and legs, her abdominal muscles will flex responsively to maintain her balance. An additional benefit to positioning your baby belly-down is that her anus faces upward. Any gas in her intestinal tract will float upward toward the anus, pushing stool along with it. If you find your baby trying to have a bowel movement, it may also help to position her knees up toward her belly, as if she is squatting.

* * *

Coughing

Newborn babies do not cough without reason, and a pediatrician should be consulted if your baby is coughing. A cough may signal an infection of the respiratory tract, an anatomic abnormality of the airways or lungs, reflux of acid and stomach contents up into the airway, or swallowing difficulty such that swallowed formula or breast milk approaches the lungs instead of the stomach. To determine the cause, your pediatrician will be interested in any additional signs or symptoms including fever, irritability, spitting up or vomiting, nasal congestion, cough frequency, or worsening of the cough when the baby is in certain positions.

* * *

Diaper rash

It is quite common for babies to develop rashes in the diaper area. The skin of the newborn bottom is very thin and sensitive. Add frequent urine and stool, held in place by a snug-fitting diaper, and it's a recipe for skin irritation and breakdown. Now consider the irritants in urine and stool: urine contains ammonia and stool is full of bile, fatty acids, bicarbonate, digestive enzymes, a variety of bacteria, and yeast. Diaper rashes can be caused by any of these substances. Most commonly, diaper rashes are simple irritation caused by the moisture, enzymes, acids and bases in the urine and stool output. Any cream or ointment that provides a barrier layer between the skin and the urine or stool output should prevent this type of irritation. Even if you missed the opportunity to *prevent* an irritative diaper rash, creams and ointments can still be helpful. Generally, thick, white creams that contain zinc oxide have more healing power for an established rash than petroleum-based ointments. Leaving the diaper off to expose the skin to air is helpful, but comes with great mess potential and is therefore impractical.

In addition to the irritants, germs that live in stool can cause diaper rashes. Any small breaks in the skin caused by friction from the diaper or irritant skin breakdown can become infected with yeast or bacteria. Identifying yeast or bacteria as the cause of a diaper rash can be difficult, but there are some clues that can help in the diagnosis:

Yeast infections occur commonly in babies because their immune systems are very immature. They are even more common, however, in babies given antibiotic medications to treat other infections. Antibiotics kill bacteria in the body, including "good" bacteria, which normally prevent yeast from causing infections. When good bacteria are killed, yeast overgrows. Yeast thrives in a very warm, moist environment (such as a diaper area) and will very often settle into skin creases or folds where two skin surfaces lay against each other. The skin becomes beefy red, and then the infection spreads outward with individual spots called "satellite lesions." If the infection continues untreated, the top layers of skin will break down and slough off. Yeast infections in the diaper area are treated with medicated anti-fungal cream, which can be prescribed by your pediatrician.

Bacteria cause infections in the diaper area when they settle into small breaks in the skin. The most common bacterial diaper infection is "bullous impetigo," caused by *Staphylococcus aureus*. Soon after the skin is infected, fragile, thin-walled blisters develop. Friction caused by the normal movement of the diaper tends to rub off the tops of the blisters, and the only evidence of infection may be circular or curved peeling edges of the blister remnants. These rashes should be treated with a medicated antibacterial cream, which can be prescribed by your pediatrician.

* * *

Diarrhea

The first newborn stool to pass (usually within twenty-four hours of birth) is called *meconium* and is dark black and sticky like tar. Over the first few days, the stool will lighten in color and change in texture. The frequency of bowel movements is variable, depending in part on the individual baby, and also on the type of milk fed to the baby. Breast-fed babies often pass stool after each feeding, whereas formula-fed babies may pass stool less frequently. The consistency of newborn stool also is variable, and may be as firm as peanut butter or as soft as pudding or mustard.

Stool that qualifies as diarrhea in a newborn usually is watery and frequent. It may soak into the diaper so that it is indistinguishable from dark urine. It may be accompanied by an increase in gas, discomfort in the abdomen, poor feeding, vomiting, fever, or a diaper rash. Babies with diarrhea generally do not gain weight well and are at risk for dehydration if too much fluid is lost through the stool output.

Causes of diarrhea in a newborn include:

1. Milk protein sensitivity – Some babies are sensitive to the proteins in milk. Infant formulas include cow milk proteins (cow casein and whey) or soy proteins. Human breast milk, in addition to human casein and whey, will also include proteins from any foods that the mother eats. Mothers who eat beef, dairy products made from cow's milk, or any products that include cow casein and whey in their ingredient list will produce milk with cow proteins. In sensitive babies who are fed cow or soy proteins, the inner lining of their gastrointestinal tract may become inflamed and irritated, and the diarrhea they develop may be bloody. These babies generally do not have fever, but may have vomiting and poor weight gain in addition to diarrhea. If you believe your baby is sensitive to milk protein, you should consult your pediatrician to discuss the possibility of switching formulas or eliminating cow or soy protein from your diet if you are breast-feeding.

2. Viral gastroenteritis – Viruses that irritate the stomach (gastro) and the intestines (enteritis) can cause diarrhea and are generally spread to babies through contaminated formula. It is always very important to prepare an infant's bottles with clean hands in a clean environment. Even if you are unaware of a "bug" circulating in the community, the germs are invisible and may be covering any surface, waiting to be picked up by someone's hands and spread around. Clues that your baby's diarrhea is caused by a viral infection include: fever, vomiting, cramping, or abdominal discomfort, excess gas, foul-smelling stool, and the presence of someone in the baby's environment with similar symptoms. Older children and adults with viral gastroenteritis tend to have milder symptoms than young babies, and may complain of only a queasy stomach, mild cramps, or loose stools. There is no medicine that will cure viral gastroenteritis, and the only treatment is to make sure the baby drinks adequate volumes of fluid during the illness. Viral gastroenteritis in a young baby can rapidly lead to dehydration through excessive fluid output in the stool or inadequate fluid intake due to vomiting or poor feeding. If the baby's stool output exceeds the fluid he is able to drink, it is likely that he will dehydrate. Your pediatrician should be contacted early in the illness, before signs of dehydration develop, including lethargy or low energy, parched, dry lips and tongue, a sunken soft spot, rapid heart rate, weight loss, and a decrease in urine output.

3. Bacterial enteritis – Bacteria cause diarrhea much less commonly than viruses, but lead to very serious disease in small babies. *Salmonella, shigella*, and *E. coli* are examples of bacteria that cause diarrhea. Like viruses, these bacteria travel in an infected person's stool and spread person-to-person, usually through contaminated food and drinks. Symptoms of bacterial enteritis may include *bloody* diarrhea, fever, abdominal pain or cramping, poor feeding, irritability, and lethargy. A newborn infected with one of these germs requires a medical evaluation, very close observation, and treatment. Your pediatrician should be contacted promptly if your newborn has symptoms of bacterial enteritis.

4. Urinary tract infection – Diarrhea sometimes accompanies infections in the urinary tract. Other symptoms may include fever, poor feeding, irritability, vomiting, and foul-smelling urine. Urinary tract infections can be quite serious if not treated, and your pediatrician should be consulted if your baby has any of the above symptoms.

5. Malabsorption syndromes – *Very rarely*, babies are born missing certain enzymes needed to digest specific nutritional substances in their milk. These babies often have difficulty gaining weight, and require specially prepared formulas to accommodate their special nutritional needs. Some of these disorders are included in the newborn screen; others are diagnosed only after the baby becomes symptomatic and is brought to medical attention.

* * *

Eye discharge

Causes of eye discharge in newborns include:

1. Eye drops or ointment placed in the eyes at the time of delivery to protect against certain infections passed from mother to baby can be irritating. Your newborn's eyes may appear slightly red or drippy soon after the drops or ointment is placed, but the irritation rarely lasts longer than twenty-four hours.

2. Conjunctivitis occurs when germs from the environment, respiratory tract, or birth canal infect the surface of the eyeball. Generally, the eye discharge is sticky and yellow and may involve one or both eyes. The skin surrounding the eye may be slightly red or swollen, but the babies are otherwise well. Your pediatrician should be consulted to evaluate the extent of the infection and prescribe antibiotic eye drops or ointment.

3. Dacryostenosis is the scientific name for blockage in the tear ducts. Our tears are produced in the upper outer corner of our eyelids. Very small tears constantly flow across our eyes to lubricate the surface of our eyeballs, and then drain into our noses through our nasolacrimal ducts. Some babies have very small ducts or ducts that are easily blocked by mucous in the nose. If the nasolacrimal duct is too small or blocked, the lubricating tears have nowhere to drain, and fall to the outside of the eye. The constant puddle of fluid that runs from the eye can pick up dust and surface particles, appearing as if it is infected. Generally, the eyeballs appear otherwise healthy, with no redness or swelling. One or both eyes may be affected, and the condition may worsen intermittently if the baby develops nasal congestion or stuffiness for any reason. Most babies will outgrow this problem as their bodies grow over the first year. If poor drainage persists after the first birthday, a pediatric ophthalmologist may need to probe the duct to resolve the problem.

4. Very rarely, a baby can be born with **glaucoma** and have a clear, runny eye discharge. Any eye discharge in your baby should be brought to the attention of your pediatrician for an evaluation.

* * *

Fever

A fever in a newborn is defined as a temperature of 100.4°F (38°C), measured rectally (review "temperature control" in chapter five to learn how to take a rectal temperature). If your baby develops a fever, you must contact your pediatrician.

In newborns, the fever itself is not the problem; the concern is that the fever is signaling the presence of an infection. Newborns have a very immature immune system, and they are considered immunocompromised. An infection in a newborn can spread rapidly throughout the body, damaging vital organ systems. In addition to fever, babies with serious infections may be irritable, lethargic, or lose interest in feeding.

Routine medical management of a newborn with fever includes sampling the baby's blood, urine, and cerebrospinal fluid (CSF) to look for infections in these sites. The blood is taken from the arm, the urine is obtained by inserting a catheter (thin tube) into the bladder, and the CSF is sampled by inserting a small needle into a space between the vertebral bones in the lower back (spinal tap). Besides the mild discomfort, these procedures are extremely low risk, and yield valuable information about the seriousness of a baby's condition during a fever. Generally, following collection of these body fluids, the baby is given antibiotics through the vein while the fluid is examined in the lab over the next few days for evidence of infection.

If other symptoms such as cough, congestion, skin rash, joint swelling, diarrhea, vomiting, or lethargy accompany your baby's fever, additional specific tests may be needed to fully evaluate your baby's condition.

In some cases, a serious bacterial infection is uncovered, and a baby requires full treatment and close follow-up. In the majority of cases, though, no serious bacterial infection is ever found. Viral infections are much more common, and fortunately far less damaging, and most babies recover fully. Occasionally, a baby will have a low fever due to excessive bundling, which will resolve when layers are removed. Those babies act otherwise well, showing no signs of illness.

* * *

Gas

Gas is common among newborns, and a common source of discomfort. The role that gas plays in the gastrointestinal tract is to assist in moving the stool forward. Intestinal muscles can move *gas* more easily than a *solid* substance; as the gas is pushed forward, the stool ahead of it moves as well. Discomfort develops when gas accumulates and stretches the intestines. Dealing with the discomfort of gas involves either reducing the amount of gas that enters the intestines, or moving the gas along more quickly.

Gas enters the belly with every swallow. Considering the newborn feeding schedule, there are lots of opportunities for gas to enter the newborn intestinal tract.

To minimize swallowed gas:

1. For bottle-fed babies, the bottle should be angled during the feeding so that the nipple is always filled with milk, not air. Some bottles are made with a built-in angle for that purpose. Other bottles use a bag system in which the air can be pushed out before the feeding, and others use a gas tube within the bottle to draw air away from the nipple area.

2. The seal of the baby's lips on the nipple should be tight and noiseless. Noise heard at the level of the lips is produced when gas is drawn into the baby's mouth between the lips and the outside of the nipple. If this occurs, try repositioning the baby's mouth to the widest part of the nipple, or consider trying a larger-size nipple.

3. Air is swallowed during crying. When your baby cries, consider his needs—feeding, diaper changing, comfort, or soothing.

4. Burping your baby throughout a feeding will release swallowed air so that it does not travel through the length of the intestines. Some babies release burps more easily than others, and you may have to experiment with different positions to determine which works best for your baby. Occasionally, a burp develops long after the end of a feeding, and your baby may signal the discomfort with crying or fussiness. An attempt at burping should always be included in the management of a fussy baby.

5. Breast-feeding mothers can avoid foods that lead to increased gas production in the intestines. Normal bacteria that live within our intestines produce gas in the process of helping to digest our food. Some foods contain substances that cause bacteria to produce excessive gas. These foods include beans, broccoli, cauliflower, cabbage, coleslaw, onions, and garlic.

To help gas move along in the intestinal tract:

1. Place your baby on his tummy on a firm surface whenever he is awake. In this position, your baby's anus is raised above the rest of his abdomen, and the gas will rise to be expelled. This position also forces him to exercise his abdominal muscles for balance when he wiggles or moves his arms and legs. The abdominal muscles squeeze his intestines, which helps to move the gas forward.

2. Massage your baby's belly gently, in a clockwise circular motion. The final part of the intestine (the colon) begins at the baby's right lower abdomen, around his hip. Peristalsis will move the gas up the right side of his abdomen toward his rib cage, then across his upper abdomen, then down his left side, before it turns slightly inward to exit at the anus. Gentle massage on the colon in the direction of flow may help to encourage peristalsis.

3. Press your baby's knees gently up into his abdomen with a bicycling motion. This activity puts gentle pressure on the intestines and exercises the abdominal muscles, which both aid in peristalsis.

Simethicone (brand names include Mylicon and Little Tummies) is an over-the-counter treatment for uncomfortable gas. It works by breaking large, uncomfortable gas bubbles into smaller bubbles that pass more easily. The liquid drops are given following each feed, up to eight times daily. It is not absorbed into the baby's body and appears to be very safe, but its effectiveness is variable.

* * *

Hiccups

It is normal for newborns to hiccup frequently. They are neither bothered nor damaged by it, and nothing should be done to interfere with the hiccups. They will stop on their own.

* * *

Irritability

Irritability in a newborn is concerning when there is no explanation for it, and if the baby is inconsolable despite the usual comfort and soothing techniques. Medically, irritability can signal the presence of serious infections whether or not it is accompanied by a fever, and it is a complaint for which your pediatrician should be consulted. Your pediatrician may ask you to measure your baby's temperature, undress your baby to look for areas of skin irritation, and review your baby's feeding, stooling and urinating pattern. It is likely, also, that you will be asked to bring the baby into the pediatrician's office for a full examination. The extent of your pediatrician's evaluation and medical management will depend on your baby's condition and your pediatrician's impression.

* * *

Jaundice

Jaundice is the yellow discoloration of skin caused by the accumulation of bilirubin, a breakdown product of blood. Babies are born with extra blood, which begins breaking down soon after birth. The bilirubin passes through the liver and exits the body with the stool (hence the bright yellow color of newborn stool). The immature newborn liver cannot process the large load of bilirubin presented to it, and the excess yellow bilirubin pigment is noticeable in the skin after two to three days. It is a normal process, which resolves over time. Occasionally, though, the excess bilirubin accumulates to very high levels, which can damage the brain. Conditions that may lead to very high bilirubin levels include prematurity, Asian race, differences between the mother's and baby's blood types, large areas of bruising or bleeding in the baby, dehydration, and infrequent stooling. Breastfeeding also may lead to jaundice after five to seven days.

Some hospital nurseries check the bilirubin level on each baby before discharge or have guidelines for monitoring bilirubin levels. If your baby's bilirubin level was not discussed with you before you left the hospital, or if your baby's skin or eyes look very yellow, or if she is not feeding or stooling well, you should contact your pediatrician. She may want to examine your baby or check your baby's bilirubin level through a simple blood test.

* * *

Lethargy

Lethargy is a condition of abnormal sluggishness and lack of energy. Although newborns spend the majority of their time sleeping, they wake to feed at regular intervals and cry vigorously. Occasionally, newborns will sleep for an extended time and not wake for an expected feeding. If your baby's nap is exceeding four hours, wake your baby and offer a feeding. If your baby accepts the feeding with interest, it is likely that he just took a long nap. A lethargic baby, on the other hand, shows little interest in his usual activities (feeding, interacting) and should be evaluated by a pediatrician for illness.

* * *

Night waking

Newborns are notorious for keeping their parents awake throughout the night. The most common sleep pattern among newborn babies is to sleep between feedings during the daytime hours and to be interactive and awake during the nighttime hours. This pattern is exhausting for parents. Many parents find that their babies sleep better at night when they are brought into the parents' bed or held on a sleeping parent throughout the night. This practice is <u>dangerous</u>. A sleeping adult is unconscious, and not in control (or unaware) of his or her actions. Many babies have been smothered, suffocated and dropped by parents who were asleep with their babies in their beds or in their arms. The very best advice is to sleep when your baby sleeps throughout the day, if possible. This schedule eventually reverses itself—hang in there.

* * *

Rashes

Your baby may develop a rash or marking that is very typical of newborn skin (see chapter two) and requires no treatment. Other rashes may develop over the first few weeks, some of which are transient, and others for which treatment is available:

1. Acne develops in babies due to the effect of maternal hormones on the baby's oil glands. The lesions are raised and red, just like pimples, and are generally limited to the face, hairline, neck, upper chest and back. Acne may be present at birth, but more often appears after several weeks, and may persist for weeks or months. There is no treatment for newborn acne, and it is best to leave the skin alone, using just water to wash the face.

2. Heat rash (miliaria or prickly heat) develops when sweat glands become blocked and irritated by heat and moisture. It appears as a collection of yellowish or red raised pinpoint-sized dots on warm, moist skin that is usually covered with clothes. Removing the clothing and allowing the skin to cool and dry is generally all that is necessary for the rash to resolve.

3. Eczema is a rough, dry, itchy rash that appears in patches or covers large areas of skin. Infantile eczema, also known as atopic dermatitis, is common in babies whose family members have allergies, and exposure to allergenic foods or substances can trigger flares. It often begins on the cheeks, but can spread to involve the skin of any body part. Eczema may develop within the first month, but more often appears after two to three months. Skin affected by eczema is dehydrated on its surface and may or may not be inflamed or infected. Therefore, the primary treatment of eczema is moisturization. Moisturizers do not *add* moisture; they *lock it in*. Thus, moisturization is best accomplished by spreading gentle moisturizer over *wet* skin. Moisturizers used on infants should be labeled hypoallergenic and should not contain any medications, menthol, dyes, or perfumes. Air humidification may help to prevent evaporation of moisture from the skin, especially in cold environments where indoor heating tends to be very dry. Inflamed eczema often appears red and slightly swollen. Food allergies may trigger the inflammatory component of eczema, and you may want to discuss the role of food allergies in your child's skin condition with your pediatrician. Topical steroids may be prescribed to treat inflamed eczema, and antibiotics may be included in the treatment regimen when the eczema appears infected, with crusting and oozing.

4. Contact dermatitis, appears as rough red patches in areas of skin that have been in contact with an irritant. Many products made for babies (soaps, shampoos, diapers, and wipes) contain chemical irritants, and switching brands may help to clear the rash. The diaper area is a common site of irritation where urine, stool, and friction from the diaper rub uncomfortably over sensitive skin. The top of the back between the shoulder blades is another common site, where clothing tags rub against the skin. Beware also of accessories, rough fabrics, and metal snaps on outfits. Usually, removal of the irritant and application of a gentle skin protectant such as A+D ointment or zinc oxide cream will allow the skin to heal. Topical steroid creams, often used in older age groups, are usually unnecessary.

* * *

Shaking and tremors

Very brief episodes of shaking, tremoring, or shivering are normal in newborn babies. The movements involve only the arms and legs, and each movement lasts only seconds. The babies are otherwise well, with good color, normal breathing, and no abnormal facial movements. As babies fall asleep, it is also common for their muscles to "jerk" briefly.

If your baby's movements are prolonged or rhythmic, or are accompanied by eye rolling, vomiting, fever, irritability, lip smacking, or sucking, consult your pediatrician. Seizures that occur in newborns may be related to chemical derangements, brain abnormalities, or infections.

* * *

Sneezing

Newborns sneeze (and hiccup) frequently. Sneezing is the body's way of clearing mucous and debris from the nasal passages. The amniotic fluid, which surrounds the baby in the womb, coats the baby's nasal passages. Additional mucous enters the baby's nose and mouth during passage through the birth canal. Frequent sneezes help to clear these fluids. Many babies also accumulate mucous and milk in their nasal passages during spitting up. You may notice congestion and sneezing in your baby if he frequently spits up. Occasional drops of normal saline into the nasal passages with or without suctioning by a bulb syringe may help to keep your baby's nasal passages flushed and clear.

Sneezing may also be part of a cold or upper respiratory infection. If your baby has a fever or is irritable, not feeding well, or coughing, you should contact your pediatrician.

* * *

Spitting up

Most babies spit up small amounts of milk at least occasionally; some babies spit up reliably after each feeding. Spitting up represents reflux of swallowed milk from the stomach back up the esophagus and out the mouth and/or nose. Simple spitting up is generally not bothersome to babies. It does not prevent them from gaining weight or developing normally, and resolves spontaneously as the baby's gastrointestinal tract matures and grows. Inadequate burping and overfeeding will make spitting up more frequent, but even good burpers who drink appropriate volumes spit up.

* * *

Thrush

Thrush is a yeast infection on the surface of the mouth. Yeast is normally present in our gastrointestinal tracts, and occasionally overgrows in infants due to their immature immune systems and frequent contact with nipples and pacifiers. Thrush appears as a white patch or speckled coating that may involve the tongue, cheeks, inner lips, gums, or roof of the mouth. Unlike milk, thrush is firmly attached to the surface of the mouth, and cannot be wiped away easily with a cloth. Your pediatrician can prescribe liquid medication and may also recommend boiling all artificial nipples and pacifiers until your baby's thrush clears up. The same liquid medication can be applied to your nipples if you breast-feed.

* * *

Torticollis (wryneck)

Torticollis usually results from a short, tight, sternocleidomastoid muscle on one side of the neck. We have two of these muscles, which originate from the bones at the top center of the chest (sternum and clavicles) and insert into the skull bones that protrude behind each of the ears (mastoid processes). Normally, flexing (tightening) one of these muscles allows us to tilt, turn, and rotate our heads to the left or right.

An abnormally short, tight muscle on one side will keep the head tilted toward the shoulder on that side, and the face and chin rotated toward the opposite shoulder. A baby with torticollis should be referred for physical therapy, a service covered by many insurance companies. Caretakers should be taught proper techniques for stretching the muscle, including head tilting and turning, carrying positions that stretch the tight neck muscle, and activities that incorporate range-of-motion exercises for the neck. Stimulating objects and toys should be placed to the baby's affected side to encourage head turning, and tummy time is helpful for these babies (while awake only). Introducing the nipple from the cheek side with the tight muscle at the start of each feeding accomplishes active stretching many times per day. Many babies find the stretching uncomfortable, but after several weeks, the muscle should begin to loosen and lengthen, eventually allowing normal movement of the head in either direction.

* * *

Vomiting

Vomiting is distinguished from spitting up by the volume and force of the regurgitated milk. Several conditions in the newborn include vomiting as a symptom, and other signs of illness may also be present. Important causes of vomiting in a newborn include:

1. **Overfeeding:** Once a baby's stomach has expanded to full capacity, it does not accept more

volume. Forced feedings will cause vomiting. Keep in mind that a baby's stomach is the size of a marble at birth, a quarter at three days and a Ping-Pong ball at two weeks. Like a balloon, it expands to accommodate a certain volume of milk. Forced beyond its capacity, however, it will overflow and cause vomiting. A very general guide to determine the appropriate volume to feed a newborn within a four-hour period is to divide the baby's weight (in pounds) by two. For example, an eight-pound baby should drink four ounces within four hours. If her feeding schedule is every two hours, she should drink only two ounces every two hours.

2. Gastroesophageal reflux disease (GERD): This condition is extremely common among newborns, but variable in its severity. It occurs in babies because the muscular ring at the top of the stomach, which should tighten after a meal to prevent the stomach contents from traveling back up the esophagus, is immature. Therefore, swallowed milk is free to slide upward and back out of the mouth. Very often, only a small portion of the milk slides upward, but large-volume vomiting can occur with severe GERD. Strategies to minimize GERD include: 1. Feed small volumes frequently to avoid overflowing a slow-draining stomach. 2. Burp your baby frequently throughout the feed since air can take up just as much space in the stomach as milk. 3. Following each feeding, keep your baby's body angled upright so that gravity helps to keep the milk low in the stomach. 4. Manage any constipation that develops, since an accumulation of stool in the intestinal tract raises the pressure that the milk must work against to flow forward. 5. Place your baby on her stomach as much as possible when she is awake. In this position, the stomach, which is in the front of our body, is kept low. Gravity then helps keep milk in the lowered stomach, and gas in the intestinal tract rises to the raised anus to be released. 6. Consult your pediatrician regarding the possible roles of antacids and the addition of infant cereal to thicken the milk in the treatment of GERD in babies.

3. Food allergy or sensitivity: Vomiting can be a symptom of a sensitivity to milk protein. The proteins in infant formulas are derived from cows or soybeans, both of which can cause allergic or sensitivity reactions. Even breast milk can contain these proteins if they are included in the mother's diet. Management of protein sensitivity requires elimination of the offending protein from the baby's diet. Switching from cow- to soy-based formula or from soy- to cow-based formula may be adequate, but many of the babies who are allergic to one type of protein are also allergic to the other. Special hypoallergenic formulas are available that provide protein in the form of very short chains of amino acids. Amino acids are the building blocks of proteins, and are recognized as foreign to the body only when they link together in long chains. Short chains still provide complete nutrition, but go unrecognized by the body. In a breast-fed baby, management of protein sensitivity requires the mother to eliminate cow proteins (casein and whey, along with beef) and/or soy proteins from her diet. If you think your baby may be sensitive to milk proteins, talk to your pediatrician about the possibility of switching formula or eliminating milk or soy protein from your diet.

4. Acute gastroenteritis: Viral infections of the gastrointestinal tract occur commonly among the general population. The viruses spread from person to person when dirty hands contaminate food. Therefore, a caretaker must *always* wash her hands and the food preparation surface before preparing a baby's bottle to prevent the spread of germs. Infected babies may have vomiting and/or diarrhea with or without fever. Contacts of the baby may have similar or milder symptoms. Babies may also be irritable, gassy, and lose interest in feeding, and are at risk for dehydration. A young baby with signs and symptoms of a viral gastrointestinal infection may be offered a water-based electrolyte rehydration solution (e.g., Pedialyte) and should be examined by a pediatrician.

5. Urinary tract infection: Infections in the bladder or kidneys may cause vomiting with or without other symptoms such as fever, irritability, or strong- or foul-smelling urine.

6. Intestinal obstruction: If milk is unable to flow through an obstructed intestinal tract, it will eventually back up and cause vomiting. Rarely, babies can be born with an obstructed intestinal tract, in which case vomiting occurs soon after feeding begins. Other intestinal tract abnormalities may go unnoticed for weeks or months before they suddenly cause an obstruction with vomiting. Vomiting due to an intestinal obstruction may be forceful. Stool output may diminish if no feedings are able to pass through; if the intestine is damaged, then bloody diarrhea may develop. Intestinal obstruction is an emergency, and vomiting, especially if it is forceful, projectile, or accompanied by abdominal distension, irritability, decreased urine output, or bloody diarrhea, should be brought to your pediatrician's attention.

7. Constipation can be so severe that a large mass of accumulated stool acts as an obstruction and causes vomiting.

8. Metabolic or chemical abnormalities: Babies with "inborn errors of metabolism," where the chemicals of the body are not in perfect balance, often develop vomiting. These are very rare disorders, some of which are tested for on the routine state newborn screen exams. Very often, other signs or symptoms such as poor weight gain, delayed development, or seizures accompany the vomiting.

10
SUPPORT SERVICES

Caring for the caretaker

Now that you know how to take care of your newborn, you need to learn how to take care of yourself—physically and emotionally.

Physical health

1. Eating well: Now, more than ever, your body needs nutrition to perform at maximum capacity. If you are postpartum, you will need to replenish lost blood, iron, and nutrients to help your body repair itself from the trauma of birth and you should discuss the need to continue a vitamin and mineral supplement with your obstetrician. If you are breast-feeding, you will need additional calories and nutrients to feed your baby. As a caretaker, you will need good nutrition to keep up with the physical demands of caring for a baby while getting less than adequate sleep. Basic nutritional principles apply—eating from all food groups, following the distribution of the old-fashioned food pyramid. Complex carbohydrates, vegetables, fruits, and proteins, including dairy products, should make up the bulk of your diet, while sweets and fats should be infrequent.

2. <u>Getting adequate sleep:</u> Although you may get enough total hours of sleep during the day, it is unlikely that those hours will be continuous and undisturbed. Multiple short naps throughout the day and night are not nearly as restful as one long night of sleep. Unfortunately, this broken pattern of sleep is the reality of newborn parenthood.
The best you can do is to sleep when your baby sleeps, and delay chores and errands that are less important.

3. <u>Exercising:</u> Regular exercise helps to restore energy and muscle tone to a tired body, and maintains good blood flow and oxygenation. If you are postpartum, your obstetrician can give you guidelines for returning to a healthy exercise routine. As a caretaker, you may enjoy exercising with your baby by taking long strolls or performing knee bends, using your newborn five- to ten-pound weight for resistance.

4. <u>Muscle strain:</u> As you handle your baby, you will feel strain in muscles you never knew existed— mostly in your back and shoulders. It is helpful to stretch frequently, reposition often, and have your muscles massaged.

Emotional health

1. <u>Depression:</u> Postpartum depression occurs in many women, and should be addressed openly between a woman and her doctor. It can interfere with the joy of parenthood, the stability of adult

relationships, and the ability of the woman to care adequately for her baby. Treatment is available, and an affected woman should discuss her treatment options with her doctor instead of suffering through the anguish alone.

2. Marriage and relationships: The addition of a new, dependent baby to your life has a tremendous impact on all of your relationships with others. If you have a spouse or a partner, you may find less time for intimacy, and you may each expect the other to do more to maintain the household. It is important to remember why you committed to your relationships before the baby joined your lives, and speak openly about the way the baby has changed your life. Difficulties in relationships are made worse with sleep deprivation, so sensitive personal topics are best discussed after a restful nap, with a clear head.

3. Sacrifice: One of the biggest adjustments to parenthood is the loss of freedom and control over your time. Babies have needs around the clock, and you will find your whole life revolving around your baby's needs. If possible, it is helpful to arrange some time for you to focus on yourself again. Hiring a babysitter or asking a friend or relative to care for the baby for a short amount of time allows you to escape the huge responsibility of baby care and feel that you haven't lost control of your own life.

* * *

Thinking ahead – preparing for the future

Alternate child care

Depending on your situation at home and at work, you may need to consider alternate child care. Even if you do not work, it is a good idea to identify people who may provide child care services should the need arise. Remember that your baby is *completely* dependent, twenty-four hours a day. If you need to leave your baby temporarily for any situation, you must arrange for alternate care. Common child care arrangements include:

Nannies provide long-term childcare services in your home. Nannies often work independently and may offer the most flexibility in the employment arrangement with the family they join. Selecting the right nanny depends on the amount of time you need child care services (days per week and hours per day), whether you want the nanny to live in your house or travel to your house each day, how much you can afford to pay, whether or not you need someone who can drive, how well the nanny's personality and child care attitudes match your own, and the responses you get from the nanny's references. You may interview many nannies before you find the best match for your situation, and are comfortable that your baby will be safe, happy, and well cared for. Referral services exist, which prescreen nannies to save you time, but charge extra fees. Legally, a nanny is an employee of your household, and you should discuss your legal responsibility with a tax consultant.

Au pairs are generally young women from other countries who provide live-in childcare services in exchange for the opportunity to spend one or two years with a host family in our country. Many different countries participate in au-pair programs, and the women are required to have a specified amount of child care experience if they will be caring for very young children. Au pairs may also have formal training in other fields, and may see the year as an opportunity to practice their English and experience American culture.

Group child care combines children from different families in a group setting to be cared for by one or more child care providers. Group childcare is highly regulated by each state, and many municipalities offer referral services to direct families to licensed and registered child care providers. Child care centers may be operated out of a private home, a separate business location dedicated to child care, or an employer or corporation that offers on-site child care to employees. The hours of operation of group child care businesses tend to be rigid; they are usually closed on weekends and holidays, and children with symptoms of illness are generally excluded until their illness resolves.

Babysitters provide child care less than full-time. Many parents make arrangements with family members, neighbors, or local people who offer babysitting services. Babysitting fees are variable and generally negotiable, and many babysitters have no formal training in child care.

Financial security

Raising a child is an expensive venture. The expense of a completely healthy baby includes feeding, clothing, baby care supplies, child care services, and routine health care visits. If your baby has an abnormality, illness, or special need, the expense is magnified. If your financial situation is inadequate to meet your baby's basic needs, consider contacting your state or county department of social services to learn what programs are available to assist you. You may qualify for low-cost or no-cost health care coverage, infant formula, or housing.

If you are fortunate to have a sound financial situation, it is never too early to plan for the future. Consider reviewing options for college savings accounts, trusts, and other savings accounts with a financial planner. Submit your baby's birth information to your health insurance plan as soon as possible; many plans require notification within thirty days of your child's birth. All new parents should meet with a lawyer to prepare wills in the event of the death of both parents. Without a will, your dependent child becomes a ward of the state in which you live, and is subject to the foster care system. Parents should also carry adequate life and disability insurance to cover the expenses of their child's dependent years.

* * *

USEFUL RESOURCES

Beware of Internet Web sites that are inaccurate and misleading—they abound! One of your best sources of information is your pediatrician, who may direct you to some reliable Web sites or local resources. The following organizations offer accurate and up-to-date information for parents:

The American Academy of Pediatrics promotes all aspects of children's health, including physical, mental, social, and environmental health. Among many features, their Web site contains a parent section, a bookstore, and a pediatrician referral service.
www.aap.org

The Centers for Disease Control and Prevention is our national health department, which functions within the Department of Health and Human Services. Information on almost any health topic can be found through a simple search, and an international travel section is useful for anyone planning a trip abroad. Advice for healthy lifestyles, injury prevention, and disaster preparedness are included on their Web site along with topics specific to childhood.
www.cdc.gov

The Immunization Action Coalition provides accurate, up-to-date information on vaccines routinely recommended in the U.S. It also discusses common vaccine concerns and vaccinations in special circumstances.
www.immunize.org

The March of Dimes focuses on preventing birth defects, promoting healthy pregnancies, and maintaining health in early infancy.
www.marchofdimes.com

The Consumer Product Safety Commission alerts consumers to hazardous products and product recalls. Their Web site includes a section on safety for kids and also allows consumers to report product safety concerns or file complaints about unsafe products.
www.cpsc.gov

The National Highway Traffic Safety Administration reviews recommendations for correct usage of infant safety seats and helps consumers determine which car seat best meets their needs. They also report safety seat recalls and can refer consumers to a local child safety seat inspector.
www.nhtsa.dot.gov

Childhelp manages a hotline providing immediate counseling and crisis intervention for distressed parents and caregivers or children at risk for child abuse. They have a database of parenting resources across the country and can make local referrals.
www.childhelp.org

The American Red Cross is a disaster relief organization. They promote disaster preparedness and also offer programs on first aid, CPR, and babysitting.
www.redcross.org

The American Heart Association is concerned with maintaining cardiovascular health through healthy lifestyles and medical care. Their Web site includes a

section on children's health, focusing on good nutrition and exercise.
www.americanheart.org

The "Infant CPR Anytime" personal learning program, offered by the American Heart Association, allows individuals and families to learn CPR conveniently in the privacy of their own home. The learning kit includes a DVD, an inflatable infant manikin with an extra lung, a reference guide, a practice phone, and sanitizing wipes.
www.cpranytime.org

Your **state or county governments** may post information for families or links to reliable resources on their Health, Education, and Social Services departments' Web sites.

Many **children's hospitals and community hospitals that provide pediatric services** will include information on child health topics on their Web sites.

INDEX